THE RAINMAKER'S 17 SECRETS TO MARKETING & ADVERTISING: ROTARY EDITION

Learn How to Earn an Additional $28,427 thru Referrals, Direct Mail, LinkedIn, YouTube, and Facebook

Attorney & Registered CPA

ROBERT SCHALLER

630-655-1233

SPEAKING ENGAGEMENTS

Attorney Robert Schaller is available to provide in-person seminars and remote webinars on a variety of topics relating to marketing, advertising, IRS back-taxes, estate planning, and bankruptcy issues.

Robert Schaller can be contacted via email at Schaller@SchallerLawFirm.com or phone at 630-655-1233. Visit Schaller's LinkedIn profile at https://www.linkedin.com/in/robert-schaller.

Dedicated to Geno Napolitano & Louie Berger,

great men

and life-long friends.

ABOUT THE AUTHOR

Attorney Robert Schaller has practiced law for more than 35 years and has generated 1,000s and 1,000s and 1,000s of clients utilizing secrets revealed in this book. He is licensed to practice in the State of Illinois. Attorney Schaller is the president of the Schaller Law Firm, P.C., and founder of the National Bankruptcy Academy and the National Offer in Compromise Academy.

Robert Schaller received his B.S. in Accountancy in 1982 from the University of Illinois at Champaign – Urbana. He received his J.D. from DePaul University College of Law in 1985 and served on the College's Law Review. He studied for an MBA at the University of Chicago in 1986. Schaller also is a Registered Certified Public Accountant.

Attorney Schaller has published the following books that are available for purchase on www.Amazon.com:

1) *The Rainmaker's 17 Secrets to Legal Marketing & Advertising.*

2) *Bankruptcy Marketing & Advertising: Learn What Every Successful Lawyer Already Knows.*

3) *Bankruptcy Selling & Closing Clients: Learn How to Persuade Prospects to Pay.*

4) *The Rainmaker's 24 Secrets to Legal Selling & Closing Clients: Learn How Successful Lawyers Persuade Prospects to Pay.*

5) *Law School Career Advisor's Resource for Starting a Solo Law Firm: Exploring a New Career Path.*

6) *Career Advisor's Guide to Starting a Solo Bankruptcy Firm: Exploring a New Career Path.*

7) *A Lawyer's Guide to Filing Chapter 7 Bankruptcy: Learning the Nuts and Bolts of Filing Your First Case.*

8) *Bankruptcy: Why My Neighbor Had to File.*

9) *DIY Guide to Filing Chapter 7 Bankruptcy: Line-by-Line Instructions and Day-by-Day Timeline.*

10) *Starting a Solo Law Firm in 2020-2021.*

11) *How to Start a Law Firm: Including a $100,000 Bankruptcy Firm.*

12) *IRS Offer in Compromise, Installment Agreements & Innocent Spouse Relief: A Treatise for Tax Professionals*

13) *IRS Innocent Spouse Tax Relief: A Treatise for Attorneys, CPAs & Tax Preparers.*

14) *IRS Installment Agreements: A Treatise for Attorneys, CPAs, Accountants & Tax Preparers.*

15) *IRS Offer in Compromise: A Treatise for Attorneys, CPAs, Accountants & Tax Preparers.*

16) *DIY Guide to IRS Offer in Compromise & The Fresh Start Initiative.*

17) *National Bankruptcy Academy's Bankruptcy MasterClass Practice System & Toolkit. Volume 1: Starting a Practice.*

18) *National Bankruptcy Academy's Bankruptcy MasterClass Practice System & Toolkit. Volume2: Marketing.*

19) *National Bankruptcy Academy's Bankruptcy MasterClass Practice System & Toolkit. Volume 3: Selling & Closing Clients.*

20) *National Bankruptcy Academy's Bankruptcy MasterClass Practice System & Toolkit. Volume 4: Client Communications.*

21) *National Bankruptcy Academy's Bankruptcy MasterClass Practice System & Toolkit. Volume 5: Processing the Petition, Schedules & Statements.*

22) *National Bankruptcy Academy's Bankruptcy MasterClass Practice System & Toolkit. Volume 6: The Bankruptcy Code.*

Schaller also published the articles below that are available online. Additional published articles are identified on his LinkedIn page.

- *Law Practice for Sale.* 2012 Illinois Bar Journal 24 (Jan 2022).

- *Yes, Income Taxes Are Dischargeable in Bankruptcy.* 2016 Illinois Bar Journal 32 (Jun 2016).

- *Bankruptcy Rule 3002(c) Filing Deadline Applies to Secured Creditors.* 2015 American Bankruptcy Institute 38 (Sept. 2015).

- *Chapter 13 Debtors Need Not Pay Late-Filed Mortgage Arrearage Claims.* NACBA Consumer Bankruptcy Journal (Winter 2015 Volume, Pages 20-24).

- *Applying the Wilko Doctrine's Anti-Arbitration Policy in Commodities Fraud Cases.* 61 Chicago-Kent Law

Review 515. (co-authored with William Lynch Schaller).

- *FSLIC Federal Receivership Appointments for Allegedly Insolvent State Savings and Loan Associations: A Plot to Federalize State Savings and Loans Against Their Will?* 33 DePaul Law Review 783.

Attorney Schaller lives in Hinsdale, Illinois with his wife Nancy. Robert Schaller's LinkedIn profile can be found at https://www.linkedin.com/in/robert-schaller.

55555

555

5555555555

555555555

5555555

Table of Contents

WHO SHOULD READ THIS BOOK?

Every Rotarian who wants to generate additional clients, build a book of business, and develop a successful business should read this book. Now, at last, the 17 secrets to marketing and advertising for professionals are revealed in one book. Professionals new to marketing can learn first-hand from a seasoned lawyer how rainmakers earn an additional $28,427 thru referrals, direct mail, LinkedIn, YouTube, and Facebook.

A professional who generates clients is called a "rainmaker." A rainmaker understands this simple truth:

Marketing = Clients = Profits = Success = Freedom

Without clients, a professional is relegated to associate status working for the rainmaker. An associate typically works for lower wages than the rainmaker, and is denied profit sharing enjoyed by the rainmaker. An associate also works at the whim and fancy of the rainmaker and lack agency to control his/her work environment, opportunities, and advancement. The rainmaker is the boss! This writing teaches an associate to become a rainmaker so he/she can become his/her own boss.

A professional often feels marketing is a daunting task – a hurdle too great to overcome. Unschooled in marketing, the professional feels intimidated and unable to take the first step. A professional must take Confucius' teachings to heart and realize that even the most difficult venture has a starting point; something which begins with the first step. Remember Confucius' saying, "a journey of a thousand miles begins with a single step." This writing is the first step of a future rainmaker's journey.

Marketing is a broad term relating to the acquisition of clients. Demographics and market research are examined in this writing because they play a big role in marketing. Demographics are the key to successful marketing. Demographic analysis is the collection and analysis of broad characteristics of past users of services. Demographers study the population on factors such as age, sex, marital status, income, child support/alimony amount of unsecured debt, number of dependents, disability, and retirement. Demographics define the universe of targeted prospects. A clear understanding of the target group is essential to effective marketing and eliminates unproductive marketing efforts and squandering of limited marketing resources.

Referrals are a key concept that is discussed from multiple dimensions, including referrals from family and friends, referrals from existing clients, referrals from fellow professionals, and referrals from in-person networking. Referral marketing may be the least expensive format with the best cost per client ratio.

Marketing thru family and friends is considered. Each professional should explain to family and friends that the professional is building a practice and needs family and friends to act like marketing "ambassadors" to help build a client base. The professional is instructed to ask these ambassadors to reach out to their contacts and spread the word that the professional practices in a specific area and can help contacts when the need arises.

Referral marketing with existing clients is examined. A strong emphasis is placed on word-of-mouth referrals given by existing and former clients. Client referrals help generate additional clients and build loyalty within the existing and former client base.

Referral marketing with fellow professionals is analyzed. A professional is urged to target those professionals who enjoy a natural symbiotic relationship with that professional. These professionals have clients who are in need of the services provided by the professional. Full-text, sample referral letters are provided so that they can be sent to other lawyers, bankers, realtors, and more.

Network marketing is also examined. Networking promotes a professional and builds solid business relationships with referrers. The resulting referrals solidify prospects' feeling of trust in the attorney personally and confidence in the attorney's abilities. Combined, they are a catalyst for building a practice. Sample networking questions and practice dialogue are provided.

Direct mail is examined because it can play a pivotal role in marketing. Direct mail allows a professional to segment the market and target those prospects most likely to need services. One of the great advantages of direct mail is that a professional can reach specific audience segments with personalized messages. The full text of successful direct mail pieces is provided.

Brochure marketing is studied in a separate chapter with a focus on the "10 Benefits of Brochure Marketing." Brochures are one of the most effective and versatile marketing tools used to inform prospective clients of the professional's services. They are simple to produce compared to other forms of marketing. Brochures are cost effective and easy to distribute. Brochure marketing is well worth adding to a professional's marketing toolbox.

Newsletter marketing is also covered in this writing with specific examples of successful campaign pieces. Newsletter marketing is the strategy by which a professional sends informational and service-focused content via U.S. mail or email to a subscriber base that compromises prospective and existing clients. Newsletter marketing is the younger sister of direct mail marketing. Newsletters are really a subset of direct mail letters, but a special chapter is warranted because of the effectiveness of newsletters in the professional arena.

Email marketing is explored in a separate chapter. Marketing professional services via email can be a fast, flexible, and cost-effective method of reaching prospects and retaining existing clients by encouraging visits to a professional's website. Email marketing allows a professional to create personalized messages to the professional's targeted audience. Emails can incorporate links to specialized landing pages to improve response rates to an email marketing campaign.

Advertising is also an important component of professional marketing. This writing considers ethical issues every professional must understand before starting to advertise for clients, including specific words and phrases that must appear in every advertising piece.

Social media is a vital part of marketing. LinkedIn is studied as a form of free marketing and paid advertising. LinkedIn is a networking tool for professionals. A professional can seek connections with other professionals to facilitate cross referrals. A professional can even find strategic marketing partners through LinkedIn. LinkedIn also helps a professional to be found when prospective clients conduct a LinkedIn search by the professional's name. Brand building is important to a professional and LinkedIn helps a professional build a brand, so the professional stands out among the bar and demonstrates his/her marketability.

YouTube is critiqued as a valuable source of free marketing and paid advertising. Creating a YouTube channel can dramatically expand a professional's marketing reach. YouTube videos enhance a professional's visibility within a highly targeted audience using limited resources. YouTube can also be used as a highly targeted, low-cost advertising platform that reaches prospects precisely when those prospects are searching for information about services the professional provides. Videos can attract prospects, share testimonials, showcase services, distinguish competitors, and offer tutorials.

Google Ads (formerly Google Adwords) search campaigns are explored with a virtual walk-through of the steps needed to start a real-life search campaign. Google Ads provides a professional with the power to reach a targeted audience with relevant advertising messages. Google Ads allows a professional to measure the results of an advertising campaign and tweak underperforming advertisements for enhanced performance. Google Ads allows a professional to maintain control of the advertising budget. The beauty of Google Ads is the immediacy of the platform. A professional can cause a display ad to appear on a prospect's search result when he/she is actively looking for professional information. This allows the professional's display ad to be shown to prospects when they are most likely to be receptive to the professional's marketing message.

Facebook advertising concludes the writing. Facebook's business "Pages" and paid ads are explored with a virtual walk-through of the steps needed to create a Facebook Page for a professional and start a real-life paid search campaign. Facebook provides a professional with the power to reach a targeted audience via free posts and with targeted advertising messages. As with Google Ads, Facebook allows a professional to measure the results of each advertising campaign and tweak underperforming advertisements for enhanced performance. Facebook allows a professional to maintain control of the advertising budget. The beauty of Facebook is its ubiquity – millions of Americans use Facebook. A professional can micromanage the targeted audience by demographic data with surprising accuracy.

In sum, professional marketing is probably one of the most vital skills a professional must develop when building a professional practice. Marketing drives a professional's image and attracts prospective clients to the firm. Successful professional marketing helps a professional stand out from the competition and helps prospects find the professional.

PART 1: THE 17 MARKETING SECRETS

SECRET 1: MARKETING 101

The American Marketing Association defines marketing as the activity and "processes for creating, communicating, delivering, and exchanging offerings that have value for customers, clients, partners, and society at large." In the professional context, marketing is the process of (1) identifying prospects who need professional services, (2) determining how best to meet those needs, and (3) developing strategies to communicate the ability to meet the prospects' needs.

Most professionals equate marketing with advertising. So, are "marketing" and "advertising" the same thing? No! Marketing is an overarching concept that includes advertising as a subset of marketing. Think of marketing as preparing a professional and his/her professional services for the marketplace. Whereas advertising is getting the word out to prospects and referral sources that the professional can provide services designed to help a targeted audience.

Subsets of marketing include:

- Market research
- Referral marketing
- Direct mail marketing
- Content marketing
- SEO marketing
- Social Media/Database Marketing
- Video marketing
- Email marketing
- Brochure marketing
- Behavioral marketing
- Influencer marketing

- Advertising
- Public relations
- Promotion
- Brand management
- And more.

Market Research

Market research is a process of determining the best audience to target and how to make a professional's service or message stand out to that particular audience. Market researchers gather information on the target market and interpret the data. Commonly used methods for information gathering include surveys, focus groups, social media monitoring, and competition monitoring.

Referral Marketing

Referral marketing is a marketing strategy that utilizes recommendations and word-of-mouth to expand a professional's client base through the networks of the professional's existing clients. Referrals provide positive information about the professional and services from a trusted source.

Direct Mail Marketing

Direct mail marketing involves sending physical pieces of promotional material via the U.S. Postal Service to a home or business. A professional utilizes direct mail to send advertising material directly to prospects included in a predefined target segment.

Direct mail offers a professional the ability to target a niche audience and to provide that audience with detailed information about the professional and the services provided. The response rate of a direct mail campaign is easily tracked to evaluate success. Direct mail campaigns can provide a high return on investment (ROI) and can be used effectively in conjunction with digital marketing campaigns.

Social Media/Database Marketing

Social Media/Database marketing is a form of direct marketing that utilizes known customer preferences and data like names, addresses, emails, phone numbers, transaction histories, customer support tickets, memberships, product orders, etc. The big difference relates to message transmission. Database marketing is disseminated via the internet whereas direct mail marketing is disseminated via the U.S. Postal Service.

Social Media/Database marketing is the strategy of leveraging customer data to deliver more personalized, relevant, and effective marketing messages to prospects. The purpose is to help a professional reach the prospects more efficiently by knowing what they want to see while allowing for the ongoing optimization of marketing efforts to boost ROI. If done effectively, database marketing allows a professional to create relevant advertising messages and meaningful experiences for prospects.

A professional is able to send targeted messages to prospects at each step of the buying process. The professional's messages can essentially "follow" the audience throughout their normal online activity. For example, a prospect has entered the term "DUI lawyer" into the Google search engine. Many professional ads appear but the prospect does nothing. The next day the prospect notices an ad for professional services in his social media newsfeed. Then he checks his email and, coincidentally, a lawyer is offering professional service for a discount! This is database marketing at its best.

Content Marketing

A professional uses content marketing to drive traffic to a website through search engine results. Content marketing is ubiquitous on the internet. Blog articles and tutorial videos are the most common examples. Content marketing focuses on creating consumable packets of information. Consumers use the information and are subliminally influenced. Effective content marketing will influence a prospect without the prospect even sensing the influence. Content marketing can build a positive connection between the prospect user and the professional provider.

Video Marketing

Video marketing is really content marketing through film. YouTube videos should immediately come to mind since the number of YouTube users exceeds 2.3 billion people worldwide.

Video marketing gives users a personal connection to what they are watching. A professional uses videos to showcase client testimonials and the attorney himself/herself. A professional can highlight features of the firm. More importantly, a professional can appeal to viewers by showing warmth, compassion, and empathy.

SEM Marketing

SEM or search engine marketing is an expansive term including both online paid search advertising and search engine optimization efforts (SEO). SEO is addressed separately below.

Paid search focuses on advertisements placed mainly on Google, since it controls 92.5% of the global search engine market. Bing, in comparison, controls only 2.5%. SEM users bid to buy ad space using targeted keyword terms relating to a professional's area of specialization. For example, "child support attorney" would be a keyword term that many prospects might enter into a Google search when seeking a divorce attorney.

As another example, Facebook advertising allows a professional to pay for ads that appear on prospects' newsfeeds of certain demographic audiences. A professional can choose the age, location, and interests of the targeted prospects. The professional's image or video will appear on the prospects' timelines.

SEO Marketing

SEO or search engine optimization relates to free advertising in search engines. SEO is the term used to label actions taken to achieve top placement in web search engine results. SEO is keyword marketing that places a marketing message on a user's computer, tablet, or phone based on specific keywords and phrases used by the user conducting the search. A key advantage of SEO is that it gives marketers the ability to target prospects with a tailored message at the time the prospect is looking for professional help.

Social Media Marketing

Social media marketing refers to the use of social media and social networks to market a firm's services through personalized public interaction. Social media marketing drives traffic to a professional's website while boosting overall firm awareness and customer loyalty. A professional achieves this by using a variety of methods on various social media platforms, from LinkedIn to Twitter to Facebook to Snapchat and everything in between. For example, the ABA Legal Technology Survey Report suggests LinkedIn is the most popular social media platform for lawyers with 57% of all law firms maintaining a LinkedIn presence. Facebook is the second most popular platform with 35% maintaining a presence.

Social media marketing provides a professional with an avenue to influence how the professional is perceived. A professional engages with existing clients and reaches new clients while allowing the professional to promote a desired culture, mission, and tone.

Behavioral Marketing

Behavioral marketing in the online space is the practice of targeting and serving ads to groups of people who exhibit similarities not only in their location, gender, or age, but also in how they act and react in their online environment. Behaviors tracked and targeted include (1) website topic areas they frequently visit or subscribe to, (2) subjects or contents or shopping categories for which they have registered, and (3) requested automatic updates or information.

Event Marketing

Event marketing is a promotional strategy that involves face-to-face contact between a professional and prospects at events like seminars, speeches, and conferences. Another name of event marketing is experiential marketing because the prospect has an experience with the professional. An insurance seminar is an example of event marketing.

Guerilla Marketing

Guerilla Marketing is a strategy in which a professional uses novel or unconventional interactions in order to promote professional services. It is a type of publicity. These methods are often low-cost or no-cost and involve the widespread use of personal interactions or through social media messaging. Guerilla marketing is all about using the unexpected to make a strong impression at public events or heavily trafficked areas.

Influencer Marketing

Influencer marketing focuses on leveraging people who have influence over a professional's prospects. A professional who uses influencers orients marketing activities around those influencers to drive a desired message to the prospects.

Influencer marketing is different from direct marketing. Direct marketing markets directly to a large group of prospects. In contrast, influencer marketing concentrates on a more focused segment of prospects that follow the influencer. The influencers are paid to spread the message on behalf of the professional. Influencers include celebrities, advocates, and content creators.

SECRET 2: MARKET RESEARCH

Demographics are the key to successful marketing. Demographic analysis is the collection and dissection of broad characteristics of past users of the same type of services the professional provides. Demographers study the population on factors such as age, sex, marital status, income, child support, alimony amount of unsecured debt, number of dependents, disability, and retirement status.

To help illustrate the importance of demographics to legal marketing, this section focuses on a lawyer who specializes in consumer bankruptcy protection. The lessons taught herein are just as applicable to lawyers who practice in other substantive areas.

DEMOGRAPHICS

The American Bankruptcy Institute, upsolve.org, fool.com, and Jonathan Fisher of Stanford University have each published an article on Chapter 7 debtor demographics that are instructive. The various demographic information gleaned from these articles is provided in separate sections below.

Understanding the demographics of Chapter 7 debtors is critical to effective marketing by bankruptcy attorneys. There are significant financial differences among male, female, and joint debtors. Joint debtors have more dependents, much higher combined incomes, higher unsecured debt levels, and are much more likely to be homeowners than either individual male or female filers. Their debt-to-income ratios tend to be a little lower than individual filers. Individual male debtors have higher incomes than individual female filers. Individual female debtors are far more likely to have dependents than male debtors.

As a group, females with no dependents had lower incomes, higher debt-to-income ratios and were more likely to be disabled or retired. The income levels of the unmarried females with dependents were about the same as the unmarried male debtors. Home-ownership rates were comparable among the three subgroups.

The Ascent published key findings about personal bankruptcy statistics at www.fool.com/the-ascent/research:

- The most common contributing factor to bankruptcy is a loss of income.

- Debtors who have completed high school or some college account for over half of all bankruptcy filings.

- Bankruptcy is more common among lower-income debtors, especially those who make $30,000 or less per year.

The Center for Economic Studies (CES) studied bankruptcy filings and found that veterans and people who are divorced, separated, and widowed are over-represented in bankruptcy, while the self-employed are under-represented. CES made the following conclusions about individual Chapter 7 filers:

- Bankruptcy filers are more likely than the general population to be employed, and to have been employed in the year preceding the bankruptcy filing.

- Bankruptcy filers are less likely than the general population to be self-employed.

- Bankruptcy filers are more likely than the general population to be divorced, separated, or widowed.

- Bankruptcy filers are more likely than the general population to be veterans.

Johnathan Fisher of Stanford University confirmed some of the conventional wisdom of who files for bankruptcy relief. Fisher compared Chapter 7 bankruptcy filers to the U.S. population as a whole and found that:

- Bankruptcy filers are more likely to be middle-aged than the U.S. population's age cohort.

- Bankruptcy filers are more likely to be middle income than the U.S. population's income cohort.

- Bankruptcy filers are more likely to be divorced than the U.S. population's divorced cohort.

- Bankruptcy filers are more likely to have terminal high school degree or some college than the U.S. population's education cohort.

Individual v. Joint Case

For this discussion, remember that bankruptcy cases can be filed by a male individually (whether married or not), by a female individually (whether married or not), or by married spouses jointly.

Jointly filed cases represent 35% of all Chapter 7 bankruptcy cases while individually filed cases represent 65% of the cases. Of those 65% of cases, individual cases filed by females represent 34% of all Chapter 7 cases. Individual cases filed by males represent 31% of all Chapter 7 cases.

Age

People aged 45-54 are most likely to declare bankruptcy. It has been reported that the average age of a bankruptcy filer was 44 years in 2007 but has increased to 48.5. One in seven bankruptcy filers (or 14%) is aged 65 or older. The bankruptcy filing rate for those aged 65-74 increased more than 200% between 1991 and 2016.

In 1991, Americans aged 25-34 filed bankruptcy at the highest rate. By 2001, those aged 35-44 had claimed the lead. Among those filing between 2013 and 2016, people aged 45-54 were most likely to declare bankruptcy. Across this same time span, the bankruptcy filing rates among those aged 18-24 and 25-34 have dropped dramatically. In short, bankruptcy is becoming less common among younger generations, and more frequent among those who are middle-aged and retirement-aged.

- 18-24: 01%
- 25-34: 12%
- 35-44: 23%
- 45-54: 32%
- 55-64: 18%
- 65 + : 14%

Sex

Bankruptcy filings by females consistently exceeds bankruptcy filings by males. Females account for 54% of filings while males account for 46% of Chapter 7 bankruptcy filings.

Another study found that bankruptcy filings by females filing individually account for 35% of the total population. Bankruptcy filings by males filing individually account for 29% of the total population. Bankruptcy filings filed jointly by married spouses account for 35% of the total population.

- Female: 54%
- Male: 46%

Race and Ethnicity

Per Jonathan Fisher of Stanford University, white people are fairly-represented in bankruptcy as compared to the U.S. population, comprising 66.8% of the bankruptcy filers compared to 67.3% of the U.S. population. Black people are over-represented in bankruptcy, comprising 14.7% of the bankruptcy filers compared to 10.7% of the U.S. population. Hispanic people are under-represented in bankruptcy, comprising 13.1% of the bankruptcy filers compared to 14.8% of the U.S. population.

Percentage of bankruptcy filers:

- White: 66.8%
- Black: 14.7%
- Hispanic: 13.1%

Education

Educational levels are divided into four categories based on the terminal degree of bankruptcy filers. A terminal degree is the term used to describe the highest level of education. The four categories are as follows: less than high school; high school; some college; and college plus.

The first three categories are over-represented in bankruptcy compared to the U.S. population and the final category is under-represented in bankruptcy. First, people who have earned less than a high school degree comprise 17.7% of the bankruptcy filers compared to 12.6% of the U.S. population. Second, people who have earned a high school degree comprise 32.3% of the bankruptcy filers compared to 27% of the U.S. population. Third, people who have earned a high school degree plus some college education comprise 35.1% of the bankruptcy filers compared to 32% of the U.S. population. Fourth, people who have earned a college degree plus additional education comprise 14.9% of the bankruptcy filers compared to 28.4% of the U.S. population.

Percentage of bankruptcy filers based on terminal degree:

- Less than high school: 17.7%
- High school: 32.3%
- Some college: 35.1%
- College plus: 14.9%

Marital Status

About 53.5% of the bankruptcy filers were married compared to 56.7% of the U.S. population. Non-married filers constituted 46.5% of the filers. Non-married filers are subdivided into two subsets: previously married and single. Previously married filers constituted 30.5% of all filers compared to 16.7% of the U.S. population. Previously married filers included filers who are divorced, widowed, and legally separated from their spouse.

The remaining single filers constitute 16% of filers compared to 26.6% of the U.S. population. However, that classification can be misleading because some "single" filers were never married while others could have mis-classified themselves as single even though they were divorced, widowed, or legally separated from their spouse. self-reported themselves

- Married: 53.5%
- Not-Married: 46.5%
    - Previously married: 30.5%
    - Single: 16%

Alimony & Child Support

Child support and alimony obligations are more common for male bankruptcy filers. Twenty-two percent of males filing individually reported paying alimony or child support. Only 2% of females filing individually reported paying alimony or child support. Nine percent of males filing jointly with a spouse reported paying alimony or child support.

- Males: 22%
- Females: 02%

Gross Income

Mean income appears to fall in the year before bankruptcy is filed. This negative shock may contribute to the need for bankruptcy filing.

The average gross income for females and males who file joint cases is $37,992. The median gross income for females and males who file joint cases is $34,632.

The average gross income for all male filers is $23,928. The median gross income for all male filers is $21,420. The average and mean are lower for unmarried male filers: $21,912 and $19,800, respectively.

The average gross income for all female filers is $19,716. The median gross income for all female filers is $18,012. The average and mean are lower for unmarried female filers without dependents: $17,112 and $15,792, respectively. The average and mean for unmarried female filers with dependents: $20,760 and $19,236, respectively.

Based on median income:

- Joint cases: $34,632

- All males: $21,420
- Males without dependents: $19,800
- All females: $18,012
- Females without dependents: $15,792
- Females with dependents: $19,236

Unsecured Debt

The average unsecured debt load for females and males who file joint cases is $44,527. The median unsecured debt load for females and males who file joint cases is $27,725.

The average unsecured debt load for all male filers is $39,928. The median unsecured debt load for all male filers is $21,925. The average and mean are lower for unmarried male filers: $35,996 and $21,700, respectively.

The average unsecured debt load for all female filers is $29,503. The median unsecured debt load for all female filers is $19,613. The average and mean are lower for unmarried female filers without dependents: $34,172 and $20,639, respectively. The average and mean for unmarried female filers with dependents: $24,953 and $17,970, respectively.

Based on median unsecured debt load:

- Joint cases: $27,725
- All males: $21,925
- Males without dependents: $21,700
- All females: $19,613
- Females without dependents: $20,639
- Females with dependents: $17,970

Debt-To-Income Ratio

The debt-to-income ratio reflects a bankruptcy filer's unsecured debt load as a percentage of the filer's annual gross income. The ratio uses two numbers. The numerator is the total priority unsecured debt added to the total non-priority unsecured debt. The denominator is the filer's annual income calculated as 12 times the gross monthly income from all sources.

Total Unsecured Debt

--------------------------- = Debt-to-Income ratio

Total Annual Income

The debt-to-income ratio for females and males who file joint cases is 91%. The debt-to-income ratio for all male filers is 104%. That ratio increases to 114% for unmarried male filers with no dependents. The debt-to-income ratio for all female filers is 123%. That ratio increases to 151% for unmarried female filers with no dependents. But decreases to 94% for unmarried female filers with dependents.

- Joint cases: 80%
- All males: 102%
- Males without dependents: 110%
- All Females: 109%
- Females without dependents: 131%
- Females with dependents: 93%

Homeownership

Homeownership or the lack of homeownership may be a key indicator of bankruptcy. Two reports vary sharply.

In the ABI report the lack of homeownership appears to be a dramatic indicator of bankruptcy. The following statistics come from this report. Male only filers lacked homeownership is 73% of the bankruptcy cases. Male only filers without dependents lacked homeownership in 74% of the cases. Female only filers lacked homeownership in 72% of the cases.

Female only filers without dependents lacked homeownership in 72% of the cases. That number increased to 75% of the cases for female only filers with dependents. Spouses who filed joint cases lacked homeownership in only 49% of the cases.

- Joint cases: 49%
- Male only: 73%
- Male only without dependents: 74%
- Female only: 72%
- Females only without dependents: 72%
- Females only with dependents: 75%

The Fisher report appears to contradict the ABI report dramatically. The Fisher report does not dissect the data into male and female statistics. Taken as a whole, the Fisher report states home ownership among Chapter 7 filers is 69.4% compared to 67.8 percent of the U.S. population. That compares to the ABI report that indicates homeownership only in the mid-20% range. Obvious more research has to be studied before the issue of homeownership can be taken as a key indicator.

Student Loans

Researchers have found that 32% of Chapter 7 filers have student loan debts. On average, student loan debt made up nearly half of their total debt. In fact, student loan debt accounted for a larger percentage of total debt across all bankruptcy filers than any other single category. The total amount of student loan debt was more than double the amount of auto loan debt, triple the amount of debt in collections, and five times as large as total medical debt.

Disability

Becoming disabled may be a negative shock that triggers bankruptcy. Chapter 7 filers that report disabilities constitute 15.3% of all bankruptcy cases compared to 10.6% of the U.S. population.

Veteran Status

Veterans are over-represented in Chapter 7 bankruptcy filings compared to the U.S. population. Veterans filing Chapter 7 constitute 12.3% of all bankruptcy cases compared to 7.3% of the U.S. population.

CAUSES OF BANKRUPTCY

Filing bankruptcy is a life event. Bankruptcy is a serious step taken by prospects suffering financial chaos. Bankruptcy cancels the chaos and offers filers a debt-free, fresh-start in life.

But what causes unmanageable debt loads. Common causes include job loss, unemployment, illness, and divorce. Consider a conducted survey of consumers who filed bankruptcy between 2013 and 2016. The survey participants were able to choose multiple factors that contributed to their bankruptcy. The most common factor chosen was a loss of income from a variety of factors. Income could have decreased because of a job loss or health issues. Decreased income could have been related to an income earning spouse's death or the divorce/separation from an income earning spouse. Below is the percentage of survey participants who "very much" or "somewhat" agreed a particular cause was a contributing factor in filing bankruptcy (note: participants could have chosen more than one factor).

- Income loss: 77.8%
- Illness:
    - Health problems: 44.3%

- o Medical expenses: 58.5%
- Divorce/Separation: 24.4%
- Spending/living beyond means: 44.4%
- Change in family size: 21.6%
- Student loans: 25%
- Tried to help friends/relatives: 28.4%

WHEN DO PROSPECTS FILE BANKRUPTCY?

Financial advisers like Dave Ramsey urge people to create an emergency fund equal to three to six months of living expenses. The emergency fund can be used to pay bills when a financial loss is suffered. Some prospects file bankruptcy file after the emergency fund has been exhausted while the financial chaos is raging unabated.

Most debtors never create an emergency fund. Some of these debtors live paycheck-to-paycheck during "good times" and save nothing for the proverbial "rainy day." When financial chaos hits, they have no safety net.

Bankruptcy becomes inevitable when the financial chaos intensifies and there are insufficient funds to solve the problem and no hope is on the horizon. With sustained unemployment, for example, the debt load strengthens unabated. Loans from friends and family become exhausted. Credit card balances are maxed out. Access to bank loans cease. The debt load builds, and pressure mounts from bill collectors and creditor attorneys.

But what is the trigger prompting a debtor to file Chapter 7 bankruptcy?

Trigger

For most prospects, bankruptcy is seen as the solution of last resort. Bank loans, family loans, friend loans come first.

Many try to budge their way out of debt by repaying over a long period of time. For others, there is no hope other than bankruptcy. But many bankruptcy prospects mimic the ostrich and put their heads in the sand fretting reality.

A trigger or negative shock sparks action and the ostrich takes its head out of the sand and contacts a bankruptcy attorney. What are some of those triggers? Life events that trigger bankruptcy include:

- Job loss
- Illness
- Divorce/separation
- Lawsuits
- Wage garnishments
- Bank levies
- Becoming disabled
- Evictions
- Home foreclosures
- Vehicle repossessions
- Student loans
- IRS liens

Job loss can trigger bankruptcy. A study by the Federal Reserve Board showed that households were 250% more likely to file for bankruptcy in the year following a job loss. Another study showed that households were 300% more likely to file in the year following a job loss.

Illness is also a trigger. More than 40% of a survey cited loss of income due to illness as a contributing factor in filing bankruptcy.

Divorce also plays a triggering role. As with the chicken and the egg dilemma, experts disagree as whether divorce causes bankruptcy or bankruptcy causes divorce. For some, the stress of financial chaos is the genesis of marital disharmony. Even strong marriages can dissolve over financial ruin. Therefore, it seems more reasonable that (1) the stress of financial chaos triggers divorce in an effort to de-escalate the marital disharmony, and (2) the divorce triggers bankruptcy in an effort to reach financial equilibrium.

THE PROSPECT'S MINDSET

Understanding a prospect's mindset is critical to market legal services effectively. The more a rainmaker understands the prospect's apprehensions, needs, and desires, the easier it is to consummate the engagement.

Apprehension

Bankruptcy prospects are not like lawyers. Attorneys are fully immersed in the world of law. For three years, law students were surrounded by soon-to-be lawyers in law school. Their professors were lawyers. Some lawyers are second or third generation lawyers. The closest friends of many lawyers are other lawyers. Some lawyers are even married to lawyers.

Not so for most bankruptcy prospects. Prospective clients are typically apprehensive about meeting bankruptcy lawyers. Remember that some prospects seeking bankruptcy protection may never have met a professional in person before. Bankruptcy prospects do not have an attorney in the family or have a friend who is an attorney. Bankruptcy prospects do not normally have a neighbor who is an attorney.

Intimidation

Few bankruptcy prospects are doctors, lawyers, engineers, bankers, or architects. These professionals are highly educated, highly trained, and highly skilled people who interact with other highly educated, highly trained, and highly skilled professionals on a regular if not daily basis.

In contrast, the typical bankruptcy prospect is far less educated, trained, and skilled. The majority of bankruptcy prospects are middle-class, lower middle-class, or working-class. That offers no indictment of them. It simply explains why they may be intimidated coming to a lawyer's office. Lacking real-world interaction with lawyers, bankruptcy prospects may rely on television stereotypes of lawyers. Prospects may view lawyers as highly competent and capable, but low in warmth and trustworthiness.

Embarrassment

Prospective clients understand their financial plight. They are embarrassed by their unfortunate financial predicament. Many believe it is their own fault that they lost a job, failed to save for a "rainy day," and failed to correctly budget the income and expenses.

Who wants to meet with a highly skilled professional and admit their deepest insecurities – and risk being ridiculed to boot? Nobody. That is why a rainmaker strives to listen closely to each prospect, show empathy for the prospect's predicament, and build trust as the foundation for client development.

Invitation Accepted

Prospective clients are not coerced into contacting a bankruptcy attorney. No appointment was ever made with a gun to any head. Instead, prospects make conscious, albeit apprehensive, decisions to reach out to an attorney for help. Prospective clients dial phones or submitted online forms with the clear goal of making an appointment.

Prospects are invited guests to an attorney's office. A lawyer offers an invitation for an initial consultation to share expertise and offer solutions. Prospects accept the offer and come to the office to reveal insecurities and find solutions.

Prospects are trying to connect. A lawyer should not fear meeting with prospects and engaging them. Rather, a lawyer should embrace the opportunity. The attorney should recognize that prospective clients are seeking help, which should be seen as a privilege to provide. The lawyer should remember that being granted a law license is a privilege and that the license should be used to help the citizenry. The fact that the lawyer is rewarded financially is just icing on the cake.

Need

Bankruptcy protection is something prospective clients need. They already know they need to file bankruptcy. Sure, there are those candidates that an attorney discovers are ineligible to file bankruptcy or whose cases would be deemed bad faith filings. But that is the minority of prospects. Seldom does a rich, highly educated, working professional with a large salary, and whopping bank account come to the office to discuss bankruptcy. A pure outlier. This writing focuses on the typical chapter 7 individual.

The important point for the attorney to realize is that bankruptcy prospects already know they need to file bankruptcy. What a gift! Few other businesses have prospects coming to their doors already knowing that they need the service. The word "selling" becomes interchangeable with the word "guiding." An attorney need only guide prospects into signing a retention agreement for bankruptcy services.

Prequalification

Prospective clients come to a legal office with the expectation that the attorney is qualified and competent to handle any bankruptcy case competently. Most prospects believe all bankruptcy attorneys are qualified and competent to handle Chapter 7 bankruptcy cases. If a prospect had any doubt as to competency of a particular attorney, then that prospect would not have made an appointment and would have chosen a different attorney.

What an advantage when it comes to convincing a prospect to engage the attorney. All an attorney has to do is confirm the prospective client's expectations.

To better understand the mindset of prospective clients, start thinking like prospects and not like a lawyer. Stop thinking of law school reputation, class rank and grade-point average. Consumer bankruptcy clients do not care. Consider the medical profession as an example. When was the last time a patient asked his/her doctor, dentist, or pharmacist what medical school the doctor/dentist/pharmacist attended, class rank achieved, or grade-point average? Probably never. And if such questions were asked, it was only asked because the patient was a lawyer who is immersed in such credentialing issues. Prospective bankruptcy clients are not similarly immersed and presume all bankruptcy lawyers are qualified.

BANKRUPTCY FILINGS BY STATE

The number of bankruptcy cases filed in 2019 equaled 749,720. The number filed in each state varied state by state. Below are the number of total bankruptcy filings in 2019 according to www.fool.com:

Alabama: 26,483
Alaska: 400
Arizona: 16,247

Arkansas:10,404
California: 67,150
Colorado: 11,037
Connecticut: 5,986
Delaware: 2,779
Florida: 45,526
Georgia: 43,046
Hawaii: 1,667
Idaho: 3,545
Illinois: 47,860
Indiana: 22,748
Iowa: 4,800
Kansas: 6,749
Kentucky: 14,882
Louisiana: 12,701
Maine: 1,327
Maryland: 17,203
Massachusetts: 7,454
Michigan: 29,387
Minnesota: 9,793
Mississippi: 12,384
Missouri: 16,852
Montana: 1,272
Nebraska: 4,021
Nevada: 9,712
New Hampshire: 1,774
New Jersey: 24,089
New Mexico: 2,997
New York: 34,683
North Carolina: 13,299
North Dakota: 720
Ohio: 36,794
Oklahoma: 9,279
Oregon: 8,601
Pennsylvania: 20,603

Rhode Island: 1,963
South Carolina: 6,790
South Dakota: 945
Tennessee: 33,305
Texas: 34,426
Utah: 9,486
Vermont: 555
Virginia: 23,071
Washington: 12,104
Washington, D.C.: 858
West Virginia: 2,779
Wisconsin: 16,364
Wyoming: 820

SECRET 3: REFERRAL MARKETING

Refferal marketing could also be known as Trust Marketing. Referrals build trust between prospective clients and the referred attorney. Consider, who do prospects trust more?

- A family member or a google search result?

- A college friend or a website banner ad?

- A professional (doctor, dentist, divorce attorney, banker, mortgage broker, realtor, etc.) or a Youtube.com video?

Naturally, prospects trust family members, friends, and professionals more than they trust google searches, banner ads, and videos. Prospects cannot help it. Their trust stems from recommendations, reviews, social app chatter, and testimonials.

But what is referral marketing? Referral marketing is a client generating strategy that utilizes recommendations, social media approval, and word-of-mouth to build a book of business through the networks of the referring sources. Many forms of referral marketing are discussed below. But in essence, referral marketing is a process that encourages a professional's contacts to evangelize the professional's abilities.

Rainmakers embrace referrals knowing word-of-mouth endorsements can drive 5x more leads than a paid web impression. Prospects acquired through word-of-mouth can convert to clients at a 10x rate of web prospects. Referred prospects that convert to clients are more likely to refer additional prospects. Most prospects would pick word-of-

43

mouth referrals if they could select only one source of information.

Marketing professor Jonah Berger identified several principles of sharing and word-of-mouth referrals in his book *Contagious*. Six principles are discussed below.

Social Currency

People refer a professional because they care about how they look to others. People share what makes them look good. Referring sources want to appear smart and knowledgeable. Bragging is the wrong word. But being in-the-know adds a gold medal to a source's social currency. Referrers who refer a professional imply some sort of connection with the professional or at least enough wisdom to know about the professional and his/her area of expertise. Who does not want to be connected in some way to an expert or specialist?

Emotion

A referring source refers a professional as an expression of care for the referred. Caring is sharing. For example, a referrer who cares about the financial wellbeing of a prospect shares the professional's contact information. The referrer knows the prospect is in legal chaos and wants to help. The best way to help is to guide the prospect towards the professional.

Rainmakers know the best way to encourage referrals is to focus on feelings rather than function. Referrers make referrals to help prospects. Referrers do not make referrals based on credentials. Therefore, a rainmaker lets a referrer know that the rainmaker is available to help the referrer's family, friends, and contacts. Rainmakers show referrers that the rainmakers care also.

Imitation

Prospects imitate the people with which they interact. There is comfort in following the crowd – especially that part of the crowd comprising family, friends, and contacts. The more public something is the more likely prospects will imitate it. Referrers who go public and disclose their own use of a professional appear genuine and compelling to prospects.

Value

Referrers share information that has practical value to others. Useful information is shared among family, friends, and contacts. A rainmaker should educate referral sources about the rainmaker's ability to help people in financial chaos. Think of a short elevator speech. A rainmaker packages knowledge and expertise so that a referrer can easily share the professional's expertise with someone in need.

Stories

Family, friends, and contacts share stories – not information. Referrers share what they have experienced, observed, or heard. Discussion about a rainmaker may travel like idle chatter. A rainmaker should position himself/herself as the focal point of the chatter. Rainmakers who advertise on TV are the best at it. However, professionals who sponsor community events come a close second. The events become the vessel in which the professionals' marketing efforts are spread.

SECRET 4: REFERRALS FROM FAMILY & FRIENDS

M om and dad are proud that their child has become a professional – so too are brothers and sisters. A member of a proud profession. But they may not know what type of service the child performs. To many, professionals are skilled in everything.

The professional should explain to family and friends that the professional is building a practice and needs the ambassadors' help in building a client base. Expressly ask ambassadors to reach out to their contacts and spread the word that the professional practices in a chosen practice area and can help those contacts when the need arises. Now is not the time to be shy. The professional needs to hone his/her talents and ability. Law school insecurities must be compartmentalized and swept aside.

The professional must educate family and friends on the types of clients served. For example, an estate planning attorney must tell ambassadors that the lawyer helps people who are creating an estate plan. However, few contacts will ask an ambassador if they know an estate planning attorney. More likely, a contact could tell an ambassador that they want to make a last will and testament. The ambassador should then be able to recognize that the contact should be referred to the lawyer.

The lawyer must also educate family and friends on the solutions provided. Using the estate planning attorney example again, the lawyer should highlight the ability to provide financially for loved-ones after death, appoint guardians for minor children, and designate someone to make health care decisions in the event of debilitation. These solutions are easily conveyed by the ambassadors.

Make Facebook the professional's friend. Ambassadors should be encouraged to post to their Facebook contacts. Plus, the professional should have a firm Facebook Page. The professional should post twice a week on social media. Most of the posts are informative and the rest community oriented. Posts should be 90% informative giving educational tips on issues relating to the attorney's practice area. The remaining 10% of posts should concentrate on local community service with the Rotary Club or other service organization.

Invite family, friends, and contacts to "like" the firm Facebook Page. This social media sharing can be much more effective than paid advertising. Social media sharing is more likely to inspire a positive interaction and get re-shared.

SECRET 5: REFERRALS FROM CLIENTS

Word-of-mouth referrals given by existing and former clients are gold. Client referrals help generate additional clients AND build loyalty within the existing and former client base.

Young professionals generally do not know how to inspire clients to refer prospects to the firm. Professionals cannot force a client to give a referral, but professionals can inspire them to do so. How?

Amazing Client Experience

Rainmakers understand that they must provide an amazing client experience to every client. Not just good, but an amazing experience. Good client service is already expected. The focus must be on providing exceptional service from client intake to case/project completion.

Let us review the client cycle and examine the various components and focus on providing exceptional service. We will start at the client intake. Clients are frequently bewildered or embarrassed about their plight. Some believe they are at fault and most do not know what steps to take.

Who wants to meet with a highly skilled professional and display their inabilities or admit their deepest insecurities – and risk being ridiculed to boot? Nobody. That is why a rainmaker strives to listen closely to each client, show empathy for the client's predicament, and build trust as the foundation for client development.

Consumer clients may also be intimidated by the attorney at the client intake. Few consumer clients are doctors, lawyers, engineers, bankers, or architects. These professionals are highly educated, highly trained, and highly skilled people who interact with other highly educated, highly trained, and highly skilled professionals on a regular if not daily basis.

In contrast, the typical consumer prospect is far less educated, trained, and skilled. Consumer prospects may be middle-class, lower middle-class, or working-class. That offers no indictment of them. It simply explains why they may be intimidated coming to a professional's office. Lacking real-world interaction with professionals, prospects may rely on television stereotypes of professionals. Prospects may view professionals as highly competent and capable, but low in warmth and trustworthiness.

A rainmaker provides exceptional service by comforting clients as if they were family or friends. The professional can keep relationships professional but still show warmth, concern, and empathy.

The same service standards should be held for every aspect of the engagement. To begin, receptionists should offer every client coffee or water upon arrival at the professional's office. The professional must walk to the reception area to greet the client instead of a receptionist bringing the client to the attorney's office. Stand and greet the client with a handshake or fist bump. Extend a warm greeting and offer body language that exudes friendliness and concern. Move the computer monitor away from the center of the desk so that there is a direct line of sight between the client's eyes and the professional's eyes. Most importantly, give the client full and complete attention. Do not answer incoming calls. Mute the cell phone. Do not look at emails. Make the client know that the intake time is bonding time. After the client engages the professional, the professional should write a handwritten thank you letter. Rarely do people get handwritten letters anymore and a handwritten thank you letter from the attorney will blow the client's mind.

Exceptional service includes continuous communication with the client. A rainmaker corresponds frequently with the client. Every case development should be shared with the client. A rainmaker shares the status of every court filing, court hearing, and conference with opposing counsel. No more than several weeks should transpire without a contact with the client. Email is great but a phone call followed by an email is better. The client does not expect such service and he/she will be thrilled to get it.

In the divorce context, contact the client ahead of any deposition and conduct a Zoom conference. Explain the purpose of the deposition and review sample questions. Inform the client as to the address of the deposition, directions, date and time, appropriate dress, and anticipated result. Discuss any proposed agreements as if the professional were talking to a brother or sister. Use everyday terms to explain complicated legal concepts. If a sister would understand, then the client would understand.

At the conclusion of an engagement, thank the client for being the "perfect" client and suggest the project was successful because of a team effort. That is how a rainmaker provides an exceptional client experience! Send another handwritten thank you note expressing gratitude for the privilege of serving the client and reinforce the successful result, and include some business cards so the client can brag to friends and family what a "great" professional the client has.

Seek a written recommendation with permission to publish it on the professional's website. Ask the client for the names of any people who the client can refer so the professional can help those people too!

A rainmaker makes the exceptional experience easily shareable on social media. Ask the client to share his/her experience on social media and put a link to the professional's Facebook Page, Twitter, and other social media apps in the email congratulating the client on the successful result. Request that the client give an online evaluation.

Continuous Client Contact

Above we discussed how to provide exceptional service so that the client will refer prospects to the professional. But the focus was on referrals given while the representation was pending.

Add a tickler to the professional's calendar as a reminder to call the client every three months after the matter was completed. Out of sight is out of mind. So, the professional must keep the attorney-client relationship in the forefront of the client's mind.

Start by entering the client's name on a CRM (customer relationship management technology) and add them to a "thank you/referral" campaign. The CRM will automatically send emails periodically thanking the client for the opportunity to serve the client and periodically requesting referrals.

Email is great, but it can be misdirected into the client's spam folder or automatically deleted by the client as duplicative. Add letters to the marketing campaign. Bi-monthly send a letter to each client letting them know how to refer a prospect by phone, email, or U.S. mail. A short, hand-written letter is best. Include a referral form and stamped, self-addressed return envelope making it easy for the client to tender a referral.

Monthly newsletters are also a must. They are easy to read, and clients tend to keep them around the house like magazines. Friends who come to visit the client can be shown the newsletters, especially during conversations centering on legal issues. Make sure each newsletter provides the professional's contact information.

Add a website referral form to facilitate referrals. The form should contain fields that request the client's name and the prospect's contact information, including name, city of residence, cell phone number, and email address. Do not make a prospect's contact information a "required" field. Partial information is okay because a partial referral prompts the professional to contact the client for the remaining information. The client's phone number would be in the attorney's records. Sometimes a client does not know the prospect's email, for example, but can give the remaining information. If all fields were required fields, then the client's efforts to refer the prospect via the website form would fail because of the lack of full contact information. A failed referral is a lost prospect and lost revenue.

The key to client marketing is staying on each client's radar and making it easy for clients to refer their friends, family, and contacts. Below is a sample client referral letter in the estate planning context.

Sample Client Referral & Testimonial Request Letter

4/16/2X

Mr. Jack Frost
1123 Main Street
Chicago, IL 60601

Congratulations on successfully completing your estate planning documents. I want to thank you for allowing me to serve you. Together we designated agents to make medical and financial decisions in the event you are unable and provided for the distribution of your assets upon death. Great job!

I know uncertainty was causing you stress but now that stress is behind you. You can get better sleep and not worry about being injured and unable to make decisions or family fighting over your belongings.

Besides helping clients obtain their legal goals, I strive to provide the best client experience possible. Please favor me with a minute of your time and complete the enclosed evaluation form. Your comments improve my efforts to provide great client care. Please tell us how be exceeded your expectation and provide any suggests on improving our service.

You can also help me in another way. Please consider referring to me a friend, family member, or contact who is in financial distress. I would be delighted to help them as I helped you. Please let them know I can help. I would be happy to explain their legal options. All consultations are free and confidential.

Also, please contact me personally with the name and address of the referral so I can help eliminate their debts and get a fresh start in life. Thank you for your time.

Sincerely,

Larry Lawyer

P.S. Please complete the enclosed evaluation form. You can mail it back to me in the enclosed self-addressed, stamped envelope.

The questionnaire should be pre-printed with the client's name and address at the top. The questionnaire questions should be:

- What is your overall feeling about your experience?

- What is your overall feeling about attorney Larry Lawyer?

- Describe a particular experience where Larry Lawyer exceeded your expectations.

- Describe any matter or procedure that could be improved upon. Include suggested improvements.

- Describe a benefit or two that you received that you value the most. Please be specific and tell us how these benefits improved your life.

Obtain the client's authorization to use the responses in the lawyer's marketing program. Add a signature line below the following language:

"By signing below, you are authorizing ABC Firm to use your name and remarks in future marketing materials.

Add a footer to the questionnaire that contains the lawyer's name, phone number, fax number, and email address. Make it easy for the client to return the questionnaire and contact the lawyer with any questions.

SECRET 6: REFERRALS FROM PROFESSIONALS

Professionals are a great source of referrals. Target those professionals who enjoy a natural symbiotic relationship with the professional. These professionals have clients who are in need of professional services provided by the attorney.

Solid referral partners are those professionals who have a dual desire to refer their clients to a professional. First, professionals are motivated to make referrals by their own self-interest. Professionals who are blocked from doing their job (and earning a commission) represent a target rich environment for a professional who can "unblock" the professional obstacles. These professionals are unable to earn commissions because of the legal chaos.

For example, consider these target-rich professional groups that are blocked from earning commissions because loans cannot be approved until toxic debts are eliminated by filing bankruptcy. They will refer prospects and thank the professional for helping both the prospects AND the professionals:

- Distressed Car dealers
- Mortgage brokers
- Realtors

Second, professionals have an ethical obligation to protect the interests of their clients, including referring clients with toxic debt loads to a bankruptcy attorney so that the debts can be eliminated. These professionals include:

- Attorneys
- CPAs, bookkeepers, and tax preparers

- Marriage counselors
- Credit counselors

Professionals typically do not have an extensive network of professional contacts. So, they have to build a network from available lists. The goal is to transform a list of strangers into a veritable referral machine.

Professionals should start a "Professional Referral Mailing Campaign" (a "PRM Campaign") to introduce themselves to prospective referral partners. A PRM Campaign casts a wide net and consists of 8 steps for each professional group. The 8-step program is described below:

Step 1: Identify a professional group that shares a natural symbiotic relationship with attorneys practicing within the professional's substantive practice area.

Step 2: Contact a list broker and lease a list of names and addresses of the professionals in the targeted group. A list is leased and cannot be resold by the attorney. Some lists can only be used once. Additional usage may require another payment.

Step 3: Create a letter that appeals to members of the targeted group. Each letter should then be customized with the specific name and address of a member. Absolutely avoid generic letters that start with "Dear Friend" or "To Whom It May Concern." These letters are discarded immediately and waste limited marketing dollars.

Step 4: Give valuable information to the targeted group. For example, give a brochure to divorce attorneys that describes the dischargeability of divorce attorney legal fees in bankruptcy.

Step 5: Mail a letter each month for three months. Use customer relationship management software (a CRM) to track the mailings and the responses.

Step 6: Include two business cards and a firm brochure.

Step 7: Subsequent letters should reference prior letters to suggestion a connection.

Step 8: Send a monthly newsletter after the third monthly letter. Use customer relationship management software (a CRM) to track the mailings and the responses.

SAMPLE REFERRAL REQUESTS – BANKRUPTCY CONTEXT

To help illustrate the motivation behind professional referrals, this chapter focuses on a lawyer who specializes in consumer bankruptcy protection. The lessons taught herein are just as applicable to lawyers who practice in other substantive areas. These lawyers would have to modify the sample letters to reflect the lawyer's substantive practice area.

Distressed Car Dealers

Car dealers make money on sales commission and repairs. The attorney should focus on the sale commissions lost because of bad credit or inability to make monthly vehicle payments due to toxic dead loads. A bankruptcy attorney should consider contacting distressed car dealers like J.D. Byrider for referrals.

J.D. Byrider allegedly targets low-income consumers with tarnished credit histories by promising quality cars, affordable loans, and an opportunity to improve their credit scores, packaged and marketed as the "J.D. Byrider Program." https://www.dotnews.com/2017/lawsuit-claims-car-dealer-

preyed-consumers-sells-poor-
product#:~:text=Byrider%20deliberately%20targeted%20low
%2Dincome,Byrider%20Program.%E2%80%9D. J.D. Byrider
has charged vehicle loan interest rates of 21%.
https://www.byrider.com/promotions/summer-savings-event-
2-3-3-2. Its website states, "When considering your
application for financing, we will look at your income, your
expenses and your budget to determine whether you qualify…
We don't just look at your credit score or how much you
make. This is one of the many reasons why customers with
less-than-perfect credit come to us. Our approval process
depends on your budget and what you can afford after you pay
your   other   living   expenses."
https://www.byrider.com/financing-and-credit/what-are-buy-
here-pay-here-loans/faq.

Here is the connection. J.D. Byrider loses the sales
commission and its share of the 21% loan revenue on each
prospect who is denied a vehicle loan because the budget is
problematic. Income may be restricted because of wage
garnishments. Expenses may be excessive because of credit
card payments, medical bill payments, and furniture rental
payments. The lost sales commission and 21% loan revenue
can be averted by a referral to a bankruptcy attorney. The
prospect files bankruptcy and eliminates the wage
garnishment, credit card bills, medical bills, etc. The prospect
is now ready to buy a vehicle from J.D. Byrider. A win-win-
win situation. The client is happy with the new vehicle and
being debt-free. J.D. Byrider is happy to have made the
referral and earned the subsequent commission. And the
lawyer is happy helping the client and being financially
rewarded for doing so.

A sample distressed car dealer letter is below:

4/16/2X

Mr. Jack Jones, President
J.D. Byrider
1123 Main Street
Chicago, IL 60601

Dear Mr. Jones:

Do you lose sales commissions when you cannot sell a car to a prospect because of budget problems, including income restrictions due to wage garnishments or excessive expenses caused by high debt loads?

What do you do with these prospects? How many more cars could be sold if those prospects had no garnishments and no debts?

My law firm concentrates its practice on helping clients eliminate wage garnishments and burdensome debts by filing bankruptcy. Generally, the firm is able to file a bankruptcy case in only a few days. Many of the firm's clients are referrals from people like you.

Clients could be eligible to buy a car from J.D. Byrider in only a few days after the referral. I would be delighted to extend a free consultation to anyone you refer. I will explain their options and benefits of bankruptcy – including the ability to obtain a car loan from J.D. Byrider after the bankruptcy is filed. Thereafter, the client would be referred back to J.D. Byrider.

Many car dealers have legal questions relating to bankruptcy. I am always available to referring dealers to answer their questions free of charge.

I would be delighted to meet you for breakfast or at the dealership to discuss how I can be of service to you and your prospects. Please have any prospect that needs immediate attention call me to schedule an appointment. I can also make available to you bankruptcy brochures for salesmen to hand to prospects who do not qualify for financing.

Sincerely,

Larry Lawyer

P.S. I have included a free copy of "The Benefits of Selling to Customers AFTER Bankruptcy." It may be of interest to you and your finance manager.

cc:

Mr. Frank Finley, Finance Manager
J.D. Byrider
1123 Main Street
Chicago, IL 60601

Mortgage Brokers

Mortgage brokers make money on real estate loan commissions. Big commissions. But the commissions depend on the ability to close a loan. Some commissions are lost because the loans cannot be closed because of wage garnishments, bad credit, toxic debt loads, lawsuits, and court judgments. The bankruptcy attorney should focus on lost sales commissions. The attorney should consider contacting mortgage brokers for referrals pitching the ability to help the brokers earn commissions on deals that would otherwise be "lost."

A sample mortgage broker letter is below:

4/16/2X

Mr. Barry Brokerski
ABC Lending Corp.

5011 N. Halstead Street
Chicago, IL 60651

Dear Mr. Brokerski:

Do you lose mortgage loan commissions when you cannot close a loan because of the borrower's wage garnishments or high debt loads? More than $10,000 per year?

What do you do with loan applicants who cannot qualify for home a loan? How much more could you earn if your clients' financial problems were eliminated?

My law firm concentrates its practice on helping clients eliminate wage garnishments and burdensome debts by filing bankruptcy. Generally, the firm is able to file a bankruptcy case in only a few days. Many of the firm's clients are referrals from professionals like you.

Clients may qualify for a mortgage loan in only 100 days after the referral. I would be delighted to extend a free consultation to anyone you refer. I will explain their options and benefits of bankruptcy – including the ability to obtain a home loan after the bankruptcy. Thereafter, the client would be referred back to you.

Many mortgage brokers have legal questions relating to bankruptcy. I am always available to referring brokers to answer their questions free of charge.

I would be delighted to meet you for breakfast or elsewhere to discuss how I can be of service to you and your prospects. Please have any prospect that needs immediate attention call me to schedule an appointment.

Sincerely,

Larry Lawyer

P.S. I have included a free copy of "Buying a Home After Bankruptcy." It may be of interest to you.

Realtors

Realtors, like mortgage brokers, make money on real closings. Big money. But the commissions depend on the buyer's ability to obtain financing and the Realtor's ability to close the deal. Some commissions are lost because the loans were not obtained because of wage garnishments, bad credit, toxic debt loads, lawsuits, and court judgments. The bankruptcy attorney should focus on lost sales commissions. The attorney should consider contacting Realtors for referrals pitching the ability to help the Realtors earn commissions on deals that would otherwise be "lost."

A sample Realtor letter is below:

4/16/2X

Ms. Betty Barnicle
Re/Home Realtors
2114 W. Jackson Blvd.
Chicago, IL 60612

Dear Betty:

Problems closing deals because buyers cannot qualify for a home loan because of wage garnishments or high debt loads?

How many more deals could you close if your buyers did not have financial problems? How much more could you earn if your buyers' financial problems were eliminated, $5,000 - $10,000?

My law firm concentrates its practice on helping clients eliminate wage garnishments and burdensome debts by filing bankruptcy. Generally, the firm is able to file a bankruptcy case in only a few days. Many of the firm's clients are referrals from professionals like you.

Buyers may qualify for a home mortgage loan in only 100 days after the referral. I would be delighted to extend a free consultation to anyone you refer. I will explain their options and benefits of bankruptcy – including the ability to obtain a home loan after the bankruptcy. Thereafter, the client would be referred back to you.

Many Realtors have legal questions relating to bankruptcy. I am always available to referring Realtors to answer their questions free of charge.

I would be delighted to meet you for breakfast or elsewhere to discuss how I can be of service to you and your buyers. Please have any buyer that needs immediate attention call me to schedule an appointment.

Sincerely,

Larry Lawyer

P.S. I have included a free copy of "Buying a Home After Bankruptcy." It may be of interest to you.

Divorce Lawyers

Divorce lawyers hear the heartache of their clients on a daily basis. The genesis of many divorces is financial chaos. A spouse loses a job and money becomes tight. A crisis occurs when the income lost is from the primary breadwinner or, worse, the sole income earner. Budgets collapse and debts explode. Spouses anxious over money problems begin to fight, escalating into separation and then divorce.

Divorcing spouses then fight over who should pay the debts. Naturally, a stay-at-home mother demands that the ex-husband pay the bills. The ex-husband may have alimony and child support to pay with little to no money left over to pay the staggering deadload. The answer, of course, is bankruptcy for both parties. Divorce attorneys know this and are happy to refer clients to a bankruptcy attorney. The bankruptcy lawyer should market to these divorce attorneys seeking referrals.

A sample divorce attorney letter is below:

4/16/2X

Mr. Andy Abernathy
Abernathy Law Firm, P.C.
219 S. Dearborn Street, 1st Floor
Chicago, IL 60604

Dear Mr. Abernathy:

Do you have family law clients in deep financial distress and need bankruptcy relief? Do you represent clients in the bankruptcy court? Please disregard this letter if you are a bankruptcy attorney too.

My law firm concentrates its practice on helping clients eliminate wage garnishments and burdensome debts by filing bankruptcy. Generally, the firm is able to file a bankruptcy case in only a few days. Many of the firm's clients are referrals from attorneys like you.

Many divorce lawyers that refer clients to us have their own concerns about the dischargeability of unpaid attorney fees once a bankruptcy case is filed. I am always available to referring lawyers to answer their questions free of charge. I have included a free copy "10 Facts Every Divorce Lawyer Should Know About Bankruptcy."

I would be delighted to meet you for breakfast or at your office, bar association, or office to discuss how I can help you and your clients. If you have any clients who need immediate attention, then please have them call me at 312-555-5555.

Sincerely,

Larry Lawyer

CPA, Accountants & Tax Preparers

A Certified Public Accountant, CPA, is a trusted financial advisor who helps individuals and businesses plan and reach their financial goals. They also counsel clients in deep financial distress. Sometimes a CPA is the first to recognize the depth of a person's financial distress.

CPAs can encounter clients in denial over their financial distress and toxic debt loads. Denial is a state where a person denies or distorts what is really happening. Deniers can ignore the problem, minimize their concern for the problem, or blame others for the financial problems. In short, denial is a powerful coping mechanism to avoid facing the truth.

CPAs do not practice denial. CPAs are number crunchers. This author is a Registered Certified Public Accountant. Numbers tell the truth and a story. Sometimes a sad story. CPAs can sometimes recognize a client's financial distress long before the client recognizes the crisis.

CPAs can be great strategic partners. CPAs are trusted by their clients and a referral from a CPA is gold. Part of the trust is transferred to the bankruptcy attorney.

A sample CPA, accountant or tax preparer letter is below:

4/16/2X

Mr. David Cpackman
Cpackman & Dorien CPAs
2458 N. Sheridan Road
Chicago, IL 60657

Dear Mr. Cpackman:

What do you do when a client is so deeply in debt that belt tightening will not help? How about when a business has failed and there is no way out?

Sometimes the CPA is the first to know the depth of the client's financial chaos. Clients can be in denial, but CPAs are trained financial experts that take action based on facts – not emotions.

My law firm concentrates its practice on helping clients eliminate debts through bankruptcy. Generally, the firm is able to file a bankruptcy case in only a few days. Many of the firm's clients are referrals from CPAs like you.

Many CPAs that refer clients to us have their own concerns about the dischargeability of unpaid fees once a bankruptcy case is filed. I am always available to referring CPAs to answer their questions free of charge. I have included a free copy "10 Facts Every CPA Should Know About Bankruptcy."

I would be delighted to meet you for breakfast or at your office, and discuss how I can you and your clients. If you have any clients who need immediate attention, then please have them call me at 312-555-5555.

Sincerely,

Larry Lawyer

Worker's Compensation Attorneys

Worker's compensation attorneys represent clients who have been injured on the job, sometimes severely injured. It is not unusual for injured workers to be unable to work due to the injury. Lost income is devastating to a family's budget. Bills mount waiting for a compensation award to materialize. It is reported that the "average case will take around 12 months, but it's not unusual for a case to take three or more years." https://www.workerscompensation.com/news_read.php?id=32814#:~:text=So%20an%20average%20case%20will,the%20insurance%20company%20won't. Eventually bills can become overwhelming to the family dynamic. Bills go unpaid, bill collectors start calling, collection actions are brought, and then bank levies – if there is anything left in the bank. Creditors do not care that the worker is not working. Promises to pay after the worker's compensation award is received do not convince creditors to backoff.

Injured workers frequently reach out to their worker's compensation attorney for a fast settlement. They need the money now! The attorney explains to the client that a settlement is a bi-lateral event and cannot be imposed upon the opponent. Moreover, the worker's compensation attorney emphasizes that the amount of a "quick" settlement could be substantially less than the award received after arbitration.

The injured attorney pleads complaining that bills are going unpaid and collection attorneys are harassing the spouse. That is the moment when the worker's compensation attorney needs to refer the client to the bankruptcy attorney to eliminate the debts and concomitant harassing phone calls and collection attorneys.

But wait. The worker's compensation attorney hesitates to refer the client to a bankruptcy attorney because the attorney is worried that the ultimate worker's compensation award would be lost to the Chapter 7 panel trustee. The question becomes: "Is a worker's compensation award protected by a bankruptcy exemption or is the award part of the bankruptcy estate subject to liquidation and tendering to unsecured creditors?" Thankfully, the worker's compensation claim is fully protected by an exemption, at least in Illinois pursuant to 820 ILCS 305/21. The bankruptcy lawyer must research the worker's compensation exemption rules in the lawyer's jurisdiction before sending the PRM Campaign letters to worker's compensation attorneys. These attorneys will not be a referral source is the compensation awards would be lost in bankruptcy.

A sample worker's compensation attorney letter is below:

4/16/2X

Mr. Carl Compenly
Compenly Law Firm, P.C.
151 S. Dearborn Street
Chicago, IL 60604

Dear Mr. Compenly:

Do you have worker's compensation clients in deep financial distress begging you to settle their claim for less than it is worth? Do you realize that the claim for worker's compensation benefits is fully exempt under Illinois law, 820 ILCS 305/21 [or insert applicable jurisdiction], and not a single penny would be lost?

My law firm concentrates its practice on helping clients eliminate wage garnishments and burdensome debts by filing bankruptcy. Generally, the firm is able to file a bankruptcy case in only a few days. Many of the firm's clients are referrals from attorneys like you.

Many worker's compensation lawyers that refer clients to us have their own concerns about the treatment of claims and other issues once a bankruptcy case is filed. I am always available to referring lawyers to answer their questions free of charge. I have included a free copy "10 Facts Every Worker's Compensation Lawyer Should Know About Bankruptcy."

I would be delighted to meet you for breakfast or at your office, bar association, or office to discuss how I can you and your clients. If you have any clients who need immediate attention, then please have them call me at 312-555-5555.

Sincerely,

Larry Lawyer

Marriage Counselors

Marriage counselors are an excellent source for strategic partnering. According to a survey by Ramsey Solutions, "money fights are the second leading cause of divorce, behind infidelity. Results show that both high levels of debt and a lack of communication are major causes for the stress and anxiety surrounding household finances."
https://www.ramseysolutions.com/company/newsroom/releases/money-ruining-marriages-in-america.

Marriage counseling comes to the rescue as a type of psychotherapy. Marriage counseling helps couples resolve conflicts and improve their relationships. Through marriage counseling, spouses can make thoughtful decisions about rebuilding the marriage and strengthening the relationship or dissolve the marriage and go separate ways.
https://www.mayoclinic.org/tests-procedures/marriage-counseling/about/pac-20385249#:~:text=Marriage%20counseling%20helps%20couples%20of,or%20going%20your%20separate%20ways.

71

Marriage counseling is often provided by licensed therapists known as marriage therapists. These therapists can have graduate or postgraduate degrees — and many choose to become credentialed by the American Association for Marriage and Family Therapy (AAMFT).

Marriage counseling is often short term. Marriage counseling typically includes both partners, but sometimes one partner chooses to work with a therapist alone.

The specific treatment plan offered by a marriage counselor depends on the situation. Sometimes a marriage counselor has a financial bent that educates and guides couples to safety. Budgeting and open communication are key. Other times, a counselor can suggest bankruptcy relief as a means of eliminating the financial chaos and toxic debt that is the heart of the couple's conflict.

Still other times, marriage counseling can be unsuccessful when the couple is in financial chaos and communication has broken down. In those cases, a marriage counsel may believe the dissolution of the marriage is inevitable. The counselor recognizes that the couple will be going separate ways.

At this point the marriage counselor can refer the patient to a bankruptcy attorney. Budgeting has failed and the future is bleak without financial relief. A separated couple divides the working couple's gross income and increases their expenses (maintaining two households instead of one). The best solution is bankruptcy relief to eliminate the financial chaos and toxic debts.

The bankruptcy lawyer should contact marriage counselors to position the lawyer as the solution to the patients' financial chaos and toxic debt.

A sample marriage counselor letter is below:

4/16/2X

Mr. Carla Counselorina
Carla's Counseling Service
4242 W. Roosevelt Road
Chicago, IL 60632

Dear Ms. Counselorina:

Do you have patients suffering with deep financial distress? How many marriages could you save if their financial chaos is eliminated?

My law firm concentrates on eliminating wage garnishments and burdensome debt loads through bankruptcy. Generally, the firm is able to file a bankruptcy case in only a few days. Many of the firm's clients are referrals from marriage counselors like you.

Many marriage counselors that refer clients to us have their own concerns about the dischargeability of unpaid fees once a bankruptcy case is filed. I am always available to referring counselors to answer their questions free of charge. I have included a free copy "10 Facts Every Marriage Counselor Should Know About Bankruptcy."

I would be delighted to meet you for breakfast or at your office, to discuss how I can you and your patients. If you have any patients who need immediate attention, then please have them call me at 312-555-5555.

Sincerely,

Larry Lawyer

SECRET 7: REFERRALS FROM NETWORKING

Face-to-face networking events are critical to client development through word-of-mouth referrals. Over 70% of consumers identify word-of-mouth referrals as a key influencer in making decisions. Do not overlook this powerful marketing component when building a practice.

Professional networking is a powerful marketing tactic. Networking promotes a professional and builds solid business relationships with referrers. The resulting referrals solidify prospects' feeling of trust in the attorney personally and confidence in the attorney's abilities. Combined, they are a catalyst for building a profitable professional practice.

There are many networking opportunities to consider. They come is various sizes and categories. Consider attending some events dominated by attorneys and other events void of attorneys. Professional events include conferences, workshops, round-tables, and of course association functions. Non-legal events include chamber of commerce gatherings, mixers, and fundraisers.

Introverts

Naturally introverted professionals can be successful networkers. EduAdvisor identifies six introverts who "changed the world": Abraham Lincoln, Meryl Streep, Steven Spielberg, Audrey Hepburn, Rosa Parks, and Albert Einstein. https://eduadvisor.my/articles /which-one-is-you-4-types-of-introverts-and-self-care-tips-to-be-your-own-hero/. Nice company to keep.

Mixing with strangers causes a discomfort or anxiety in introverts. Introverts fare better at networking events when they prepare for events in advance. Advanced planning helps minimize the discomfort. Introverts must be ready for the key question:

"What type of professional are you?"

Every introvert should have a 30-second elevator speech ready to go. An elevator speech is a clear, brief messages or "commercial" about the professional. It communicates who the professional is, what type of client the professional is looking for, and how the professional can benefit a prospect. Elevator speeches are typically 30 seconds, the time it takes people to ride from the top to the bottom of a building in an elevator.

The professional needs to imprint his/her "brand" upon a prospective referrer. A personal brand is the unique value a professional brings to the table that benefits prospective clients. Communicating a brand is an effective way to demonstrate the professional's professional aptitude, strengths, and skills. It also lets referrers know exactly the type of prospect the professional is seeking. In 30 seconds, a fellow networking professional would know whether a symbiotic relationship is possible.

Introverts should come to a networking event ready to listen more and talk less. Quantity of interactions is not the goal; quality connections is the goal. Truly listen without interrupting, losing focus, or, worse, looking at a cell phone.

Prospective referrers also have an elevator speech to communicate. Try to remember the four key pieces of information disseminated by the prospective referrer:

1. Who: Name of prospective referrer.

2. What: Type of client the referrer is looking for.
3. How: Benefits the referrer's clients receive.
4. Why: Potential for symbiosis.

Symbiotic relationships are mutually beneficial. The referrer must get something in return for giving a referral. Analyze each prospective referrer with the goal of developing a symbiotic relationship. Those relationships survive the test of time. A one-way relationship is fleeting. For example, a divorce attorney could be a referral source to an estate planning attorney. A divorce attorney has clients who are divorcing and may need to revise their last will and testament. In return, the estate planning attorney has clients who may be considering divorce. A referral to the divorce attorney would pay dividends.

Next, introverts should prepare questions in advance, including icebreakers. The focus of each interaction is to provide an elevator speech and to digest prospective referrers' elevator speeches as discussed above. But it can be awkward going straight for the meat. Awkward interactions can enhance an introvert's discomfort and anxiety. Icebreaking questions offer great transitions. Remember to use questions and not statements. Questions expand conversations while statements stifle them.

Here are some icebreaking questions to memorize:

"How long have you been a part of this organization?"

"Have you attended one of these events before?

"Do you know anyone else here?"

"What do you do?"

"What are some of your favorite projects you are working on right now?"

"What are some challenges you are facing right now?"

For estate planners: "Would any of your clients benefit by estate planning?"

For bankruptcy lawyers: "Would any of your clients benefit by eliminating their debts and getting a fresh start in life?"

For personal injury lawyers: "Have any of your clients been injured as a result of another person's fault?"

Introverts should expect awkward moments during every networking event. It is inevitable. Not every attendee is a polished conversationalist. Some professionals can be rude and intentionally exclude an introvert from conversations. Some networking events are comprised of people who know each other well – like a chamber of commerce event. Attendees familiar with each other can congregate in small pods and be unwelcoming to newcomers. Introverts who are newcomers to a group should avoid those pods and target other newcomers or individuals standing alone. The food table and drink station are good places to meet individuals. Everyone likes food and drink, and it is an easy place to spark a conversation.

The cell phone can be a friend or foe. As a friend, the cell phone allows professionals to swap contact information via text. The iPhone has a "Share Contact" link on each contact. By clicking the share contact link an introvert can forward his/her contact information to a fellow professional. It goes both ways, the professional can forward similar contact information to the introvert. As a foe, the cell phone can discourage other attendees from approaching the introvert. For example, it is not uncommon for an introvert to pull out a cell phone when nobody is talking to the introvert. It avoids embarrassment, but it discourages anyone from approaching the introvert. If embarrassed, an introvert is better offer going to the restroom and emotionally regrouping or going back to the drink station. Remember, the goal of attending a networking event is to build a sustainable professional practice and not revisit a high school party with cliques.

Introverts can stick to a fellow attendee for too long. Remember, attendees came to the networking event to meet other professionals and not just one professional. In fact, an introvert who gloms onto another professional can be destroying the very relationship the introvert is trying to ignite.

The secret to furthering a successful contact is to suggest a post-event plan and then to disengage and circulate to another attendee. The post-event plan could be a breakfast meeting, a cup of coffee, or a zoom chat depending on the circumstances. Hand a business card to the attendee and move to the next person. Introverts should have a few disengagement statements in their quiver. Consider these:

"It was great meeting you. But I promised to talk to a few people before I leave. I look forward to our breakfast meeting."

"It was my pleasure talking with you. I think we could really help each other. I know you have other people to talk to. Before I go, can you point me in the direction of a divorce attorney? I promised myself I would meet two divorce attorneys today."

The attendee will not be insulted. In fact, he/she will probably be impressed with the professional's networking skills. The professional concludes the interaction on an upbeat note and moves on to engage another attendee.

Attitude & Habits

A professional needs to establish internal motivators to succeed in networking. A networker must develop the right behaviors and habits. Building solid networking behaviors starts with a professional making a commitment to finding success in client development. Positive behaviors affect a professional's networking attitude. A negative attitude breeds a negative result. A positive attitude propels a professional to honor the networking commitments made by the professional to himself/herself.

The professional should establish a networking routine. For example, each Saturday morning the professional should set aside two hours for client development. The first Saturday focuses on networking habit formation and skill development, networking goals, and networking opportunities.

During the first hour, a networking calendar should be created for opportunities and commitments. The professional should Google networking events tailored solely for attorneys (like bar association events) and events that are only tangentially related to attorneys (like chamber of commerce events). Online registration is available for many events. Next, a list of prospective referrers should be created with dates and time identified for contacting the referrers. This process should be repeated every Saturday morning.

During the second hour, the professional should evaluate his/her weekly performance. Did the professional contact the prospective referrers as scheduled on the calendar? Be harsh. Identify networking opportunities missed and evaluate the reason they were missed. Break bad habits by labeling the habit and changing the routine that fosters the bad habit.

Reinforce a positive attitude and make another weekly commitment to form good networking habits. Promote a mindset that networking is enjoyable, a key to building a successful professional practice. Enjoyment, really? Yes! Think of networking as a means to an end – a positive end. A successful practice pushes profit. A successful practice promotes pride in oneself. Now focus on enjoying the process of networking instead of the labor of networking.

Targeted Events

A professional's time is limited so effective time management is critical to success. But how does a networker determine which audience to target?

A perfect event hosts a networker's targeted audience. But the concept of a perfect person is a fantasy. There is no one perfect person that will build a burgeoning professional practice. Instead, networkers target three groups of people. The first group contains the direct buyers of professional services – aka prospective clients. The second group comprises symbiotic or strategic partners who can refer prospects who need professional services provided by the professional. The third group consists of influencers who may direct a professional to strategic partners.

The professional should create a list of events attended by prospects. Events might include church, Alcohol Anonymous meetings, Gambler's Anonymous meetings, and financial management seminars.

The professional should create a master list of professionals and non-professionals who interact with prospects. The list should identify job titles and services provided by those professionals to prospects. The list could include divorce attorneys, marriage counselors, bank loan officers, and accountants.

These lists help a networker identify networking events worth targeting. The professional can quickly determine if a networking event will be fruitful or is disqualified as unproductive. Researching an event starts with internet browsing and is followed by a short conversation with the organizers or someone who has attended the event before. Questions to ask the organizers include:

"How many people do you expect to attend the event?"

"How many professionals will be attending the event?"

"How frequently are these events presented?"

"Are there any opportunities for the professional to speak as an educator?"

These lists also help networkers identify organizations worth joining. It takes valuable time to successfully infiltrate an organization for networking purposes. Strategic partners are developed through mutual participation. So, it behooves the professional to determine the professional makeup of any organization under consideration.

It is critical to ask questions in advance to learn the goals of the organization and makeup of its committees and board members before investing irretrievable blocks of time. Ask questions like:

"What is the professional makeup of the committee/board members?"

"Are there any divorce attorneys, accountants, loan officers, or loan officers on the committee/board?"

"When are meetings held?"

"Are there any other professionals on the committee or board?"

Identifying target-rich environments is difficult for a professional. The best way to start is to ask senior professionals with admirable business development skills for recommendations on the best avenues for finding prospects. Most professionals would be flattered by the question and honored to share ideas. Start with the committee members of the local bar association.

Sometimes new professionals do not know any senior professionals who will share their knowledge. Those professionals should investigate which events are attended by bigwigs. Research will reveal which organizations, boards, and charities movers and shakers focus their time.

Networkers should consider organizations in which they share a personal interest or common cause. A charitable organization or law school group could inspire a professional to expand networking efforts. Networking can be exhausting but networking with people who share a common interest or cause could transform that exhaustion into inspiration.

Networking Plan

Planning is the key to success. Professionals need a business plan. Professionals need a marketing plan. Networkers need a networking action plan. Benjamin Franklin is credited with saying, "If you fail to plan, you are planning to fail."

Networkers look at the big picture. Nothing great is ever accomplished overnight. A 12-month time horizon should be the starting point to set objectives. Then activities should be divided into quarterly, weekly, and daily tasks.

Network planning is as simple as 1-2-3. Step one is to set the primary objectives for the next 12 months. Specific objectives should be identified. For example, a networker could plan to develop five strategic partners who are accountants, another five who are divorce attorneys, and five more who are marriage counselors. That is 15 strategic partners over the next 12 months or 1.25 strategic partners per month. A very doable objective.

Step two of the networking plan relates to the game plan or strategies to be employed to implement the primary objectives. A good start includes attending conferences, workshops, round-tables, and professional functions. But be more specific in the networking plan and identify opportunities that will facilitate interaction between networkers and prospective strategic partners.

Minimize time spent on events that are saturated with other attorneys practicing in the same field. The committee of the local bar association is probably the last place to get referrals. Instead, focus efforts on events that will maximize exposure to prospective strategic partners.

Step three of the networking plan requires networkers to identify specific tasks to be performed. These tasks answer the who, what, where, and when questions. For example, networkers can meet divorce attorneys at family law committee meetings at the local bar association. Everyone there will be a divorce attorney. Almost every divorce attorney wants to know if estate planning documents must be revised upon divorce. Be the expert or the go-to-attorney on all things estate planning [or insert issues relating to the lawyer's substantive area].

Networkers can meet accountants at AICPA sponsored events like the EDGE Conference or offer to speak at the AICPA Leadership Academy on a topic relating to the lawyer's field. Networkers can speak to marriage counselors at conferences hosted by the American Association for Marriage and Family Therapy (AAMFT) or the state associations like the Illinois Affiliation of Marriage and Family Therapists (IAMFT).

Those specific tasks should be calendared. Some say nothing gets done without it being on the calendar. Think of the times someone fails to workout at the gym because they got too busy and did not add time on the schedules to exercise. Calendars help keep track of networking events and track due dates on tasks to be performed. Calendaring motivates networkers to stay on their networking schedule. Finally, calendaring eases networking anxiety and prevents feeling overwhelmed by client development. Remember the saying, "a journey of a thousand miles begins with a single step." A single step is not so bad.

Below is an example of the first part of a networking action plan for residential real estate attorneys.

Strategy 1: Develop five strategic partners who practice divorce law and represent clients who may need the services of a real estate attorney.

Tactic 1: Develop an "elevator speech" tailored to divorce attorneys.

- Draft an elevator speech that is 30 seconds long.
- Identify a band or niche that affects divorce attorneys, like representing divorcing husbands who will be selling investment real property.

- Specify the type of referrals at issue, like wives or husbands.
- Describe the benefits of selling investment real estate.
- Establish that reciprocal referrals are anticipated.
- Deadline: 30 days.

Tactic 2: Create a "reverse elevator speech" that asks open-ended questions and probes a divorce attorney's likelihood of being a strategic partner.

- Draft a reverse elevator speech that consists of 5 questions.
- Determine whether the attorney specializes in divorce law or only has a handful of cases.
- Identify the number of pending divorce cases the attorney is handling.
- Inquire as to frequency of selling real estate by the attorney's typical divorcing client.
- Ask about the typical equity in homes and net worth (asset value less secured debt) of the attorney's typical divorcing client.
- Ask the attorney if he/she currently has a relationship with a real estate attorney to give referrals and receive divorce referrals.
- Deadline: 45 days.

Tactic 3: Research committees and events where targeted professionals congregate.

- Speak with other professionals to better understand which committees and events are best to meet professionals with clients who may need professional services.
- Research local associations for list of targeted professionals and dates/times of committee meetings.

- Contact the committee chairperson to discuss format, number of attendees, and opportunity to speak on real estate law issues relevant to divorce attorneys.
- Deadline: 60 days.

Tactic 4: Attend events twice a month and meet 2 divorce attorneys at each meeting.

- Speak to four attorneys at each meeting.
- Ask each divorce attorney if he/she currently has a relationship with a real estate attorney to give referrals and receive divorce referrals.
- Ask for a business card from each divorce attorney.
- Grade each targeted professional with an A, B, or C relating to the potential to be a strategic partner.
- Promise a follow-up action with A and B lawyers.
- Deadline: monthly.

Tactic 5: Speak at one event each month as a real estate expert or write one divorce-related real estate article for a bar journal.

- Contact bar association committee chairmen (state, city, county bar associations) proposing a topic of interest to divorce attorneys.
- Obtain permission to disseminate a "real estate paper" to committee attendees on divorce-related real estate issues.
- Contact bar journals' editorial boards for article submission guidelines.
- Deadline: monthly.

Tactic 6: Communicate with prospective strategic partners met at the event.

- Within 24 hours of event, calendar task to contact each prospective partner.

- Within 48 hours of event, contact each prospective partner as promised.
- Discuss the event with the prospective partner and schedule a follow-up in-person meeting to build rapport.
- Deadline: 24-48 hours.

Constantly evaluate the effectiveness of the networking action plan. The action plan is only a plan after all – it is not a commandment. An underperforming plan should be modified as needed until perfected. Modification comes from analysis. Weekly analysis is best.

The networker must chart everything to track progress, including:

- Number of committee meetings attended.
- Number of speeches scheduled/conducted at bar associations.
- Number of articles submitted to bar association journals.
- Number of "real estate papers" disseminated at bar association committee meetings.
- Number of strategic partner interactions.
- Number of A-list strategic partner follow-up phone discussions within 48 hours of events.
- Number of B-list strategic partner follow-up phone discussions within 48 hours of events.
- Number of follow-up in-person meetings with strategic partners.
- Number of referrals from strategic partners.
- Number of new clients resulting from referrals.

Only through measurement can networkers evaluate progress. Underperforming networkers must determine the reason for the underperformance. Underperformance can be the result of an overly ambitious networking action plan. More likely, underperformance is associated with procrastination and intentional avoidance. Overperforming networkers should pat themselves on the back and increase the aggressiveness of their networking action plans. After all, networkers can never have too many strategic partners or too many clients!

Elevator Speech

The goal of a networking elevator speech is to broadcast a networker's value to a prospective strategic partner in 30 seconds so that the strategic partner wants to continue the conversation. An impossible task for unprepared people who attend networking events intending to "wing it to see what happens." Advanced preparation is the key.

An elevator speech is divided into five parts. Each part should be honed to perfection. The first part begins by identifying who the networker is and what the networker does. For example, consider saying,

"Hello, my name is Joe Smith. I'm a personal injury lawyer helping people receive full compensation for their injuries."

The second part of an elevator speech describes the networker's ability to alleviate a client's pain points. Do not focus on the professional process; instead, focus on the client's pain. A discussion of pain alleviation grabs the attention of prospective strategic partners. Partners immediately and instinctively consider whether their clients have similar pain points that could also be alleviated by the networker. Consider saying,

---

"My typical client has suffered a catastrophic physical injury as a result of someone else's carelessness."

An elevator speech should be tailored to the targeted audience using emotional words that paint a vivid picture. As another example, the speech above could be tailored for divorce attorneys as follows:

"My typical client has marital problems and is deeply in debt. Fierce fighting with the spouse over unpaid bills is not unusual. So are collection nightmares like wage garnishments, bank levies, vehicle repossessions and foreclosures. What a mess."

The phrase "marital problems" triggers a response or relevancy in divorce attorneys. "Fierce fighting" is nice alliteration suggesting irreconcilable conflict. The phrase "collection nightmares" paints a disturbing image. Ending with "what a mess" indicates the magnitude of the client's financial chaos.

The third part of an elevator speech identifies a differentiator that makes the networker unique or at least separates the networker from other attorneys. But what is a differentiator? Rainmakers develop a message that is different from other personal injury attorneys yet compelling enough to the needs of prospective strategic partners. For example,

"My subspecialty is helping the non-injured spouse receive compensation for loss of consortium."

The fourth part of an elevator speech is an invitation extended to prospective strategic partners to take the next step towards forging a mutually beneficial relationship. The invitation opens the door for a longer conversation if the networker's skills can help the prospect's clients. Consider the following,

"If you are interested in hearing more about how I help clients struggling with catastrophic injury, I can email you some YouTube videos if you give me your business card. Or I would be delighted to contact you in a few days to discuss it over the phone. Would you like that?"

This call to action requires the prospective partner to make a decision. A prospective partner could give a clear buying signal that a strategic partnership could be mutually beneficial. On the other hand, if the partner sees no benefit in continuing, then the answer would probably be "No, thank you" or "I don't think my clients would have a need for your type of help." It is a polite response and a clear signal that the prospective partner is not a match. The networker should thank the person for his/her time and ask to be directed to anyone who has clients who may need a personal injury attorney.

The fifth part of the elevator speech occurs only when the prospective partner is interested in working together. Then, the networker must ask an open-ended question prompting the partner to give his/her elevator speech with a tangential focus on the lawyer's area of practice.

"Now it's your turn. Tell me what you do and whether any of your clients would benefit by talking to a personal injury attorney?"

Developing Rapport

Rapport is defined as a close harmonious relationship in which two people are in sync with each other, understand each other's feelings or ideas, and communicate smoothly. Developing rapport with a total stranger at a networking event is not an easy task. It takes work. Hence the root word "work" in the term networking.

Thankfully, rapport can be established when two willing networkers are skilled in the art of networking. Remember that networkers attend events for the purpose of networking. Both should be skilled in the art of communicating with prospects. Both should understand the feeling of anxiety associated with "working a room" of strangers. But it would not be called work if it is easy.

Networking is easier when the networker is prepared with a list of questions to ask prospective strategic partners. Ask questions and listen. Listen 80% of the conversation and talk 20%. People love to talk about themselves and anxious people feel more comfortable talking about the topic they know best – themselves. Good listeners foster meaningful relationships. A good listener is perceived as a wise person, who can understand and empathize with others.

Get the contact talking by asking open-ended questions. Yes/No questions can kill a conversation. Start with questions about the contact's business: name, location, number of professionals/employees, length of time working for the business.

Expand the conversation and ask the contact how he/she decided to work for the business. Ask the contact to identify the tasks she likes most about his/her current position. Find out what makes the contact get out of bed in the morning. Ask for an example of a completed project that brought joy to the contact.

Shift the focus and inquire about professional frustrations. Everyone has them. Ask what changes the contact would like made to make the job more satisfying. This question allows the contact to open up and bond with the networker. Display empathy. Determine whether the networker has any power to help the contact or knows any person who may be able to help the contact. A friend when in need is a friend indeed.

Ask about the contact's career story. Where did the contact work before the current job? How did that job prepare the contact for the current job? What is the contact's professional background? Ask about college and graduate school when talking to contacts and inquire how their school(s) helped prepare the contact for the "real world."

Rapport is enhanced when sharing personal interests as well. Ask what the contact does for fun on the weekends. Ask about pets. Everyone loves their own dog or cat. Everyone has a pet story. Inquire into hobbies. People love to talk about their hobbies. If lucky, a networker can bond when sharing a common hobby like bike riding or golfing.

Finally, ask about the contact's hometown and seek a connection. Any mutual friends or acquaintances from that hometown? Ask about what the contact likes best about the hometown and surrounding area. Ask the contact to recommend tourist attractions if the networker would ever visit the area.

In essence, rapport is fostered by showing interest in the contact's professional and personal life. Allow a contact to connect with the networker by taking interest in the contact's stories and understanding how the prospect feels. The best way to connect with someone is not by talking, but by listening.

Post Event Follow-Up Phone Conference

The networking event went great, and the networker met a hot prospect who the networker hopes will be a source of future referrals. The networker graded the prospective strategic partner as an A+ prospect based on the interaction during the networking event.

The networker must contact the prospect within 48 hours after the networking event as promised. A 15-minute phone conference is more efficient than a lunch meeting. Time is money and there is not enough time in the day to meet with everyone. The phone conference helps qualify the prospect for strategic partnership purposes. Only qualified prospects are invited to lunch to cement the relationship.

The networker should prepare questions ahead of the phone conference to help qualify or disqualify the prospect as a strategic partner. The key issue is whether the contact's goals and abilities align with the networker. The contact should be disqualified if the contact already has a strategic partner to whom the contact sends professional referrals. Similarly, the contact should be disqualified if the contact demonstrates that the contact is a "taker" whose goal is to take referrals from the networker but not to give any in return. Reciprocation is mandatory. Also, the contact should be disqualified if the contact is new to networking and has few people in the contact's networking pool. None of these disqualifying factors suggests the contact is a bad person – only that the contact is an inappropriate strategic partner.

Questions to ask during the follow-up phone conference include:

"How long have you been practicing [law or insert other profession]?"

"How do you evaluate prospective strategic partners?"

"What networking activities do you pursue?"

"What type of referrals do you typically give other than [insert lawyer's substantive area] referrals?"

"Who are you currently partnered with to receive referrals?"

"How long have you been partnered with that source?"

"Who are you currently partnered with to give [insert lawyer's substantive area] referrals?"

"How long have you been giving [insert lawyer's substantive area] referrals to your current partner?"

"Are the people you referred to the [insert lawyer's substantive area] lawyer happy with the referrals? What has been the feedback?"

"How many [insert lawyer's substantive area] referrals to you expect to give every month?"

An in-person meeting should be scheduled by the networker once the contact is deemed qualified during the post event follow-up phone conference. The in-person meeting should be one-on-one.

Post Event One-On-One Meeting

The one-on-one meeting is best conducted in a quiet setting. A breakfast or lunch at a neutral location can be effective as long as the tables are sufficient spaced for privacy. A fast-food restaurant must be avoided – too much noise and too little privacy. A meeting at the lawyer's office works best because a lawyer's office oozes professionalism and competence – exactly what the prospective strategic partner wants to feel.

The one-on-one meeting is a professional meeting, so treat it that way. Prepare questions in advance as was done for the phone conference. Prepare an agenda in advance too. Send a copy of the agenda to the contact ahead of the meeting to show organization, professionalism, and efficiency. An agenda shows the contact that the networker's goal is to evaluate the viability of strategic partnering and not merely to make a new friend.

Start the live meeting by exchanging common pleasantries. Build rapport by moving to a positive anecdote of the networking event at which the contact was met. Then get down to business. Start by reminding the contact of the time parameter set during the post event phone conference. The parameter defines the length of the meeting and puts pressure on the contact to be efficient. Say,

"We agreed on the phone that we would meet for 60 minutes today. Does that still work for you?"

Next, the networker should turn off the cell phone and ask the contact to do likewise. The impression given is that the contact is the most important matter to the networker and demands full attention. The contact's reciprocal act of turning off the contact's cell phone is an implied agreement.

Then, ask the contact if the contact has read the agenda sent in advance and ask "permission" to discuss the first topic. This minimizes the unproductive preliminary chatter. Plus, the contact would have a hard time declining the networker's suggestion without appearing rude. Instead, the contact would almost certainly grant the networker permission to start talking business.

The first item on the agenda is to define the purpose of the meeting. The networker must make it clear that the purpose is to determine the viability of strategic partnering. Use more welcoming language, like,

"I'm looking for a win-win relationship. The purpose of this meeting is to determine if there is a good fit between us. I am looking for a mutually beneficial relationship. Are we in agreement?"

The second item on the agenda is setting the structure of the meeting. Vocalize the expectation that both will learn about each other's business and referral needs. Set a 10 or 15-minute time frame and politely give the contact the choice of going first. The stated time parameter reduces the risk that the contact will be unfocused and absorb more than a fair share of the meeting time and feel the need for another meeting to hear about the networker's law practice and referral needs. Start with the following,

"Let's start with you spending about 10-15 minutes telling me about your business, what services you provide to help people, and the type of person you are looking to get referred to you. Then I'll do the same. Sound okay?"

Be ready with a list of prepared questions to help qualify the contact as a strategic partner. Consider these questions:

"How would you describe your clients?"

"What makes your service unique and how do you differentiate yourself from your competition?"

"Who are your main competitors?"

"What referral sources work best for you?"

"What type of referral are you looking for from me?"

"How important is it to you that the attorney you refer is competent and professional?"

"How many other networking partners do you work together with?"

"Are you currently working with any [insert lawyer's substantive area] attorneys as a strategic partner? If so, who are you connected with?"

The one-on-one meeting should be concluded on a high note. An understanding that working together would not be a fit can be a positive outcome, albeit not the outcome hoped for coming into the meeting. Thank the contact for his/her time and understand that disqualifying the contact after the first meeting saves time wasted on future meetings. Cut bait and move on.

On the other hand, the better outcome would be the recognition that there is a good fit between the contact and the networker. The connection is now made. Build slowly to build the bond. Do not rush in and present a contract to sign obligating the contact to refer clients. That would doom the relationship. Instead, communicate a feeling that there is a good fit.

Offer to make a connection for the contact to a third-party but emphasize the quid pro quo of the relationship. Conclude the meeting by suggesting a small step together like another one-on-one meeting or attending some social event together. These suggestions allow the contact to confirm the contact's feeling that there is a good fit.

SECRET 8: ETHICS IN ADVERTISING

Check with a ethics expert before you start advertising. Certain professions have restrictions, rules, and regulations on advertising. For example, advertising is a relatively new phenomenon in the history of the legal profession. Until 1977, lawyers were prohibited from advertising. That all changed when the United States Supreme Court issued its opinion in *Bates et al v. State Bar of Arizona*, 433 U.S. 350 (1977). The *Bates* decision charged legal marketing forever.

Then, for the first time, lawyers could directly communicate with prospective clients and offer their services. But lawyers' efforts to communicate directly with prospects is still limited by and rules of professional responsibility promulgated by licensing entities.

Lawyer advertising is held to a higher standard than laymen advertising. Best practices suggest creating every advertisement with the expectation that every ad will be scrutinized by the state ethics review board. Always keep this expectation in mind when implementing the advertising campaign. Doing so will keep the lawyer from accidentally meandering into trouble.

Advertising – State Limitations

Virtually all state licensing rules limit the lawyer's ability to advertise. Attorneys must familiarize themselves with advertising limitations contained in their state licensing rules. In Illinois, for example, lawyers are generally prohibited by the Illinois Rules of Professional Conduct (I.R.P.C.) from soliciting professional employment by in-person, live telephone, or real-time electronic contact when a significant motive for the lawyer's contact is the lawyer's pecuniary gain. I.R.P.C. § 7.3(a). Every written, recorded, or electronic communication from a lawyer soliciting professional employment from anyone known to be in need of legal services in a particular matter shall include the words "Advertising Material" on the outside envelope, if any, and at the beginning and ending of any recorded or electronic communication, unless the recipient of the communication is a person specified in paragraphs (a)(1) or (a)(2) of I.R.P.C. § 7.3.

A solicitation is a targeted communication initiated by the lawyer that is directed to a specific person and that offers to provide, or can reasonably be understood as offering to provide, legal services. In contrast, a lawyer's communication typically does not constitute a solicitation if it is directed to the general public, such as through a billboard, an internet banner advertisement, a website, or a television commercial, or if it is in response to a request for information or is automatically generated in response to Internet searches.

There is a potential for abuse when a solicitation involves direct in-person, live telephone, or real-time electronic contact by a lawyer with someone known to need legal services. These forms of contact subject a person to the private importuning of the trained advocate in a direct interpersonal encounter. The person, who may already feel overwhelmed by the circumstances giving rise to the need for legal services, may find it difficult to evaluate fully all available alternatives with reasoned judgment and appropriate self-interest in the face of the lawyer's presence and insistence upon being retained immediately. The situation is fraught with the possibility of undue influence, intimidation, and over-reaching.

This potential for abuse inherent in direct in-person, live telephone or real time electronic solicitation justifies its prohibition, particularly since lawyers have alternative means of conveying necessary information to those who may be in need of legal services. In particular, communications can be mailed or transmitted by email or other electronic means that do not involve real-time contact and do not violate other laws governing solicitations. These forms of communications and solicitations make it possible for the public to be informed about the need for legal services, and about the qualifications of available lawyers and law firms, without subjecting the public to direct in-person, telephone or real-time electronic persuasion that may overwhelm a person's judgment.

The use of general advertising and written, recorded or electronic communications to transmit information from lawyer to the public rather than direct in-person, live telephone, or real-time electronic contact, will help to assure that the information flows cleanly as well as freely. The contents of advertisements and communications permitted can be permanently recorded so that they cannot be disputed and may be shared with others who know the lawyer. This potential for informal review is itself likely to help guard against statements and claims that might constitute false and misleading communications. The contents of direct in-person, live telephone or real-time electronic contact can be disputed and may not be subject to third-party scrutiny. Consequently, they are much more likely to approach (and occasionally cross) the dividing line between accurate representations and those that are false and misleading.

There is far less likelihood that a lawyer would engage in abusive practices against a former client, or a person with whom the lawyer has close personal or family relationship, or in situations in which the lawyer is motivated by considerations other than the lawyer's pecuniary gain. Nor is there a serious potential for abuse when the person contacted is a lawyer. Consequently, the general prohibition in Rule 7.3(a) and the requirements of Rule 7.3(c) are not applicable in those situations. Also, I.R.P.C. § 7.3(a) is not intended to prohibit a lawyer from participating in constitutionally protected activities of public or charitable legal-service organizations or bona fide political, social, civic, fraternal, employee or trade organizations whose purposes include providing or recommending legal services to their members or beneficiaries.

But even permitted forms of solicitation can be abused. Thus, any solicitation which contains information which is false or misleading, which involves coercion, duress, or harassment, or which involves contact with someone who has made known to the lawyer a desire not to be solicited by the lawyer is prohibited. Moreover, if after sending a letter or other communication the lawyer receives no response, any further effort to communicate with the recipient of the communication may violate the provisions of Rule 7.3(b).

The requirement in I.R.P.C. § 7.3(c) that certain communications be marked "Advertising Material" does not apply to communications sent in response to requests of potential clients or their spokespersons or sponsors. General announcements by lawyers, including changes in personnel or office location, do not constitute communications soliciting professional employment from a client known to be in need of legal services.

So, the bottom line is that some advertising is allowed by the rules of professional conduct. However, be certain to review all advertising materials carefully for false exaggerations. Ethics boards hold lawyers to a higher standard than the standard required by the Federal Trade Commission and other governmental agencies. But where is the fine line between misleading and "puffing?" Banks and car dealers can claim they are the best or offer the best deal; lawyers should never make such a claim if they want to avoid scrutiny.

A lawyer must not make a false or misleading communication about the lawyer or the lawyer's services. I.R.P.C. § 7.1. A communication is misleading if it contains a material misrepresentation of fact or law, or omits a fact necessary to make the statement considered as a whole not materially misleading.

I.R.P.C. § 7.1. This rule governs all communications about a lawyer's services, including permitted advertising. Whatever means are used to make known a lawyer's services, statements about them must be truthful.

Truthful statements that are misleading are also prohibited. A truthful statement is misleading if it omits a fact necessary to make the lawyer's communication considered as a whole not materially misleading. A truthful statement is also misleading if there is a substantial likelihood that it will lead a reasonable person to formulate a specific conclusion about the lawyer or the lawyer's services for which there is no reasonable factual foundation.

An advertisement that truthfully reports a lawyer's achievements on behalf of clients or former clients may be misleading if presented so as to lead a reasonable person to form an unjustified expectation that the same results could be obtained for other clients in similar matters without reference to the specific factual and legal circumstances of each client's case. Similarly, an unsubstantiated comparison of the lawyer's services or fees with the services or fees of other lawyers may be misleading if presented with such specificity as would lead a reasonable person to conclude that the comparison can be substantiated. The inclusion of an appropriate disclaimer or qualifying language may preclude a finding that a statement is likely to create unjustified expectations or otherwise mislead the public.

Illinois lawyers are also prohibited from stating or implying an ability to influence improperly a government agency or official or to achieve results by means that violate the Rules of Professional Conduct or other law. I.R.P.C. § 8.4(e).

Illinois lawyer advertising must include the name and office address of at least one lawyer or law firm responsible for its content. I.R.P.C. § 7.2(c).

I.R.P.C. § 7(b) prohibits a lawyer from giving anything of value to a person for recommending the lawyer's services except that a lawyer may: (1) pay the reasonable costs of advertisements or communications; (2) pay the usual charges of a legal service plan or a not-for-profit lawyer referral service; (3) pay for the purchase of a law practice; and (4) refer clients to another lawyer or a nonlawyer professional pursuant to an agreement not otherwise prohibited under these Rules that provides for the other person to refer clients or customers to the lawyer, if (i) the reciprocal referral agreement is not exclusive, and (ii) the client is informed of the existence and nature of the agreement.

To assist the public in learning about and obtaining legal services, lawyers should be allowed to make known their services not only through reputation but also through organized information campaigns in the form of advertising. Advertising involves an active quest for clients, contrary to the tradition that a lawyer should not seek clientele. However, the public's need to know about legal services can be fulfilled in part through advertising. This need is particularly acute in the case of persons of moderate means who have not made extensive use of legal services. The interest in expanding public information about legal services ought to prevail over considerations of tradition. Nevertheless, advertising by lawyers entails the risk of practices that are misleading or overreaching.

This Rule permits public dissemination of information concerning a lawyer's name or firm name, address, email address, website, and telephone number; the kinds of services the lawyer will undertake; the basis on which the lawyer's fees are determined, including prices for specific services and payment and credit arrangements; a lawyer's foreign language ability; names of references and, with their consent, names of clients regularly represented; and other information that might invite the attention of those seeking legal assistance.

Questions of effectiveness and taste in advertising are matters of speculation and subjective judgment. Some jurisdictions have had extensive prohibitions against television and other forms of advertising, against advertising going beyond specified facts about a lawyer, or against "undignified" advertising. Television, the internet, and other forms of electronic communication are now among the most powerful media for getting information to the public, particularly persons of low and moderate income; prohibiting television, internet, and other forms of electronic advertising, therefore, would impede the flow of information about legal services to many sectors of the public. Limiting the information that may be advertised has a similar effect and assumes that the bar can accurately forecast the kind of information that the public would regard as relevant.

State supreme courts or their designated licensing agents have mechanisms to enforce their state licensing rules. Enforcement could range from censure, reprimand, suspension, or disbarment. So, study the licensing rules relating to advertising and take them seriously. Design every advertising piece as if will be scrutinized by the ethics police – because if a lawyer is ever under the ethics police's microscope the advertisement will be scrutinized closely.

Advertising – Federal Limitations

Some advertising limitations have been imposed by Congress. Research must be conducted to determine whether any federal laws or regulations apply to a lawyer's substantive area.

For example, Congress has placed advertising limitations upon bankruptcy lawyers. *See* 11 U.S.C. §528. These limitations are in addition to, and not an alternative to, the advertising limitations provided in any state's rules of professional conduct. Congress imposed restrictions on any advertisement directed to the general public that indicates that the bankruptcy lawyer provides assistance with respect to credit defaults, mortgage foreclosures, eviction proceedings, excessive debt, debt collection pressure, or inability to pay any consumer debt.

What restrictions? First, bankruptcy lawyers must "clearly and conspicuously disclose in any advertisement of bankruptcy assistance services or of the benefits of bankruptcy directed to the general public (whether in general media, seminars or specific mailings, telephonic or electronic messages, or otherwise) that the services or benefits are with respect to bankruptcy relief under" the Bankruptcy Code. 11 U.S.C. § 528(a)(3).

Second, bankruptcy attorneys must "clearly and conspicuously use the following statement in such advertisement: 'We are a debt relief agency. We help people file for bankruptcy relief under the Bankruptcy Code.' or a substantially similar statement." 11 U.S.C. § 528(a)(4).

Third, bankruptcy lawyers must disclose clearly and conspicuously in any advertisement that the lawyer's assistance may involve bankruptcy relief under the U.S. Bankruptcy Code. 11 U.S.C. § 528(b)(2)(A). Also, bankruptcy lawyer advertisements must include the following statement: "We are a debt relief agency. We help people file for bankruptcy relief under the Bankruptcy Code." --- or a substantially similarly statement. 11 U.S.C. § 528(b)(2)(B).

Congress also defined what is meant by a bankruptcy advertisement. The Bankruptcy Code states that an advertisement of bankruptcy services or of the benefits of bankruptcy directed to the general public includes—(A) descriptions of bankruptcy assistance in connection with a Chapter 13 plan whether or not Chapter 13 is specifically mentioned in such advertisement; and (B) statements such as "federally supervised repayment plan" or "Federal debt restructuring help" or other similar statements that could lead a reasonable consumer to believe that debt counseling was being offered when in fact the services were directed to providing bankruptcy assistance with a chapter 13 plan or other form of bankruptcy relief under Title 11 of the U.S. Code. 11 U.S.C. §528(b)(1).

Like the state supreme courts, the bankruptcy court has a mechanism to enforce the U.S. Bankruptcy Code's advertising rules. The charges can be brought by the United States Trustee's Office via a motion for sanctions. A bankruptcy court would rule on the motion for sanctions. Enforcement could range from censure, reprimand, suspension, or disbarment from practicing bankruptcy law. Best practices suggest studying the Bankruptcy Code's advertising rules and take them seriously. Design every advertising piece as if will be scrutinized by the U.S. Trustee.

SECRET 9: DIRECT MAIL MARKETING

Direct mail is a marketing strategy that involves sending physical letters, postcards, mailers, or brochures to prospective clients via the U.S. Postal Service. Direct mail marketing is a form of communicating an offer, where a professional communicates directly to a pre-selected demographic group and supplies a method for a direct response to the professional. Direct mail is relatively easy to do when following the upcoming discussion of targeting, personalization, and creativity.

Benefits of Direct Mail

Direct mail allows a professional to segment the market and target those prospects most likely to need the professional services provided by the professional. One of the great advantages of direct mail is that a professional can reach specific audience segments with personalized messages. For example, a direct mail message to prospects suffering from wage garnishments would be different from a direct mail message to prospects suffering from foreclosure or vehicle repossession.

Direct mail is a marketing channel that is tangible and engages all the senses. A prospect can ever touch and feel it. Many people actually want to receive direct mail marketing messages. Consequently, direct mail has been reported to be over 5x more likely to be remembered than digital channels. Research strongly suggests that consumers trust brands from direct mail much more than digital ads.

Direct mail "open rates" exceed email open rates. Prospects' attention to direct mail has increased as more and more businesses turn to digital advertising. The mailbox has become less crowded and less competitive. The result is more attention per letter. Research shows that 82% of direct mail is opened and 47% of direct mail is read or skimmed.

Response rates are better with direct mail than email. The response rate of a successful direct mail campaign can be between 2.7% to 4.4%. *See* https://www.designdistributors.com /blog/14-key-benefits-of-direct-mail-marketing. This dwarfs email response rates, which can be as low as 0.12% response. Many people delete emails from solicitors without even opening them.

Direct mail can reach the entire household. Research shows that the average piece of mail is kept in the household for 17 days. It is shared on average with members of the house 23% of the time. Some prospects wait months contemplating professional action before action is actually taken. A physical direct mail piece can be retained by the prospect for months until the prospect deems action necessary. Moreover, some professional issues can be discussed between spouses. In those cases, the direct mail piece can be shared between spouses.

Personalized direct mail works the best. People do not receive as much mail as they used to and look favorably on mail which is humanized. Personalized letters must include the name of the prospects. Do not use "To Whom it May Concern." Also, weave additional personalized information into each letter or postcard. For example, if a prospect's wages are being garnished, then include the name of the judgment creditor, amount of the judgment, and court that enforced the judgment. Research indicates exponential performance increases with three or more personalization points.

Direct mail is creative and versatile. Direct mail offers greater creative options compared to digital alternatives. Online banner and social media ads enable photo and text changes, but size is usually standardized. Email is limited by only one line of text being visible to users before they choose to open or delete the emails.

Another benefit of direct mail is the ability to highly target prospective clients. Acute attention to demographics drives the success rate of direct mail. Open rates and ROI are directly related to demographics. The more tailored the demographic scope, the more effective the direct mail campaign.

Disadvantages of Direct Mail

Cost is the primary disadvantage of direct mail. Direct mail has variable costs relating to postage, printing, and mailing lists. Postage costs are the leading deterrent to direct mail. Letters and flats are expensive when you start multiplying the individual postage piece rate by thousands. For example, postage for a first-class mail letter is $0.55 and the total cost of mailing 1,000 pieces would be $550. The printing costs vary based on size and weight of the paper and envelopes. Printing costs can be minimized by using standard size letters and envelopes with without colored ink, but the effectiveness may also be minimized. A cost benefit analysis must be conducted. A higher open rate relating to a high profit margin business like personal injury may increase the ROI. For example, an extra $150 in cost should be embraced if it results in an extra personal injury fee of $51,995. Mailing lists are discussed below.

Life Cycle of a Direct Mail Campaign

Every direct mail campaign begins with a demographic study of people needing professional services offered by the professional. The professional needs to understand who is being targeted. Markets can be segmented based on need and based on events causing a person to need professional representation.

The second step is to obtain a mailing list once the demographics are discerned. The mailing list must contain the names and addresses of the targeted population of course. But additional information is relevant. Three or more personalization points increase performance exponentially.

The third step is to create the ideal mailing. Should a postcard be sent or a personalized letter? Every mailing must be personalized. For example, if a prospect's home is being foreclosed, then include the name of the foreclosing bank (e.g., Chase Bank), name of the court and judge if known (e.g., Circuit Court, Judge Jones presiding), case number (e.g., 2021 CH 12345), and location of the court (e.g., Middle District of Tennessee). Consider the subject line, text font, text size, and the call-to-action. Nothing should be random. Every aspect of the mailing must be considered.

The fourth step is to add a code number that is unique to each direct mail campaign. A unique code allows a professional to precisely measure the results of a campaign. ROI can be calculated when the professional knows the number of new clients obtained from each campaign. ROI would determine whether the campaign should continue, be tweaked for better performance, or terminated.

The firth step relates to testing the campaign. Direct mail campaigns should be split tested. Split testing is also known as A/B testing. A/B testing is a process of delivering two variants of the same direct mail piece at the same time and comparing which variant drives a better response. A/B testing helps professionals identify less productive mailings and directs limited advertising resources to more productive mailings.

A/B testing increases ROI based on short-term inquires, long-term client creation, or other important metrics.

The sixth step is to prepare for responses to the direct mail campaign. Have the professional's website ready for action if the direct mail piece directed prospects to the website – for a free eBook for example. Have the professional's receptionist ready for action if the direct mail directed the prospect to call the professional's office to make an appointment for a free consultation.

The seventh, and final, step is to analyze the results of the direct mail campaign. How many people landed on the professional's webpage and downloaded the free eBook? How many prospects contacted the professional's office and scheduled a free consultation? How many of the leads turned into paying clients? Which of the several versions of the direct mail piece was most effective? Think about why one version was more successful. Use conclusions to improve the next campaign.

Response Tracking with Direct Mail

Direct mail responses must be tracked to evaluate performance. There are a variety of techniques that help professionals measure campaign performance.

a. Tracking by unique code.

A unique code is added to each direct mail campaign. The code must be easy to locate by a prospect. It can be helpful to insert the code after each prospect's name on the address line, in a special box that is easily located, or at the top or bottom right-had corner of the direct mail piece. Each prospect must be able to find the code easily and communicate the code to the professional, receptionist, or webpage.

b. Tracking via a website.

One of the most common tracking methods for a direct mail campaign is to use a custom landing page and list the URL on your direct mail campaign. A less common, but effective, tracking method is to create a custom personalized URL that redirects users to an existing page pre-populated with the prospect's data. This makes the experience much quicker and simpler. Personalized URLs help identify landing page hits and recipient actions.

c. Tracking via custom phone numbers.

Unique phone numbers can be created for each direct mail campaign to forward and document calls to those numbers. Custom phone numbers enable a professional to understand what marketing methods resulted in the best response rate.

d. Tracking via exclusive offers.

Professionals can create an exclusive offer for a direct mail campaign. Then the professional can track the number of contacts requesting the exclusive offer. Further analysis would determine the number of contacts who engaged the professional after seeking the exclusive offer.

e. Tracking via QR codes.

QR codes redirect prospects to the professional's website where the users' actions can be tracked.

Postcard Usage

The obvious difference between a postcard and a letter is visibility. The postcard message appears on the front and back allowing prospects to see the offering immediately. Letters are concealed in an envelope.

Postcards must have a clear bold headline that outlines exactly what problems the professional's service solves. For example, "Stop your wage-garnishment in 24 hours." is an effective headline that allows a prospect to understand the lawyer's offer with just a glance at the postcard. The prospect would not have to second guess the appeal or read the remainder of the card to understand the offer.

Every postcard must have an "ask" informing prospects of what action should be taken next. Does the professional want prospects to call the office requesting an appointment? How about visit the professional's website to obtain a free eBook? Postcards should end with a clear direction on what prospects should do. Keep it short and punchy. Use the "ask" multiple times to reinforce the action. For example, end with the direction, "Phone 312-555-5555 today to stop the wage garnishment tomorrow."

Image is key. A postcard's image must be crisp and clear to grab prospects' attention. Use popping colors that will stand out. The image used on the front of the postcard has two purposes: grab attention, and communicate what the postcard is about. Avoid the common mistake of only focusing on one or the other. An attention-grabbing image (e.g., an appeal to sex) unrelated to the professional's service is distracting and detrimental to the success of the campaign. An uninspiring picture (e.g., picture of a law library) communicating the lawyer's message is also not helpful. For example, an image of a judge's gavel on top of a paycheck stub or on top of a pile of money could be magical.

Each postcard campaign must include an offer that acts as bait to encourage prospects to take action. Think from the prospects' point of view instead of the professional's point of view. What offer would actually trigger prospects' decision to take action?

Postcard substance should focus on the benefits of contacting the professional and not on the features. "Sell the sizzle and not the steak" is a common expression in sales. Prospects do not buy features, they buy benefits. For example, a prospect filing bankruptcy does not want a reduced credit card balance; that prospect wants a debt-free, worry-free, fresh start in life. Consider this example, "Stop worrying about money problems, we can help you generate more cash by terminating the wage-garnishment."

Contact information must appear on the postcard. Name and address are mandatory. The big decision to make is whether to include the professional's phone number, email address, web address, or all three. A phone number alone directs the prospect to the professional's receptionist. Some people like personal attention when a receptionist answers the phone; however, some people shy away from personal contact and would prefer to schedule an appointment via an online calendar portal. An email address alone forces prospects to communicate via the internet.

A professional would have longer to respond to emails than to phone calls, but a prospect may call a competitor while waiting for the professional to respond to the email. Last, a web address (URL) alone is effective when the professional wants to direct prospects to the professional's landing page, which may expand on the offer made on the postcard as well as a calendaring software to self-schedule a free consultation. The URL approach is best used when the professional only wants clients who are internet savvy. Most professionals would probably opt for adding all three to the post card: phone number, email address, and web URL. Thus, allowing prospects to make their own choices.

Postcards should contain only one message. Space is limited so drive the prospect to take a clearly defined action.

Over-communicating leads to confusion and the prospect's inaction. Professional can be verbose. Professionals must fight the urge to use 100 words when 20 can say the same thing with more marketing punch. Tighten the language and use language recognizable by the prospects. No legalese!

Letter Usage

Letters can be superior to postcards when the mailing requires a more official or personal touch, or needs to explain a lot of information. A letter from a law office is uncommon for most people. The mere appearance of prestige may cause a prospect to open the letter.

Another advantage of letter marketing is the space it gives the professional. The professional has room to display his/her bona fides. If the professional's services require more explanation and details (such as how organizing a business as an LLC is better than incorporation), a letter gives the professional more space to explain benefits and solutions.

The larger page area also gives the professional the chance to convey a more comprehensive message, demonstrating to prospects that the professional is invested in them, through effective storytelling or targeted appeals to emotion.

Furthermore, a professional can implement many different direct mail strategies with a letter and envelope to better convey a sense of importance and capture the prospect's attention. These methods include hand-addressing a letter or using a pen-addressing machine. In addition, snap pack mailers are often used to convey important messages because of their unique design.

As we briefly discussed above, letters are slightly more expensive than postcards because of factors like envelope style and design, but that slightly higher price point can be worth it for advertisements that are more informative, personalized, and professional.

A Successful Strategy

Every successful direct mail strategy begins with identifying the goal. As an example, let us assume a criminal defense lawyer's goal is to drive prospects to an online sales funnel. This strategy motivates prospects to visit the lawyer's website and provide their names and contact information for follow-up selling. Closing the deal is not part of this direct mail strategy – closing is a separate strategy explored elsewhere.

a. Mailing List

A professional must identify the market segment that will be targeted. For this strategy, the target market is a divorced man, 35 to 45 years old, arrested for DUI.

b. Format

A professional should not feel the need to reinvent the wheel. Look at what competitors are doing in terms of formatting. Are competitors using postcards, letters, invitations, coupons? Competitors are not uninformed. Seasoned competitors may have been using a particular format for years because it delivers results. Consider utilizing the same format and tailor the marketing piece to the professional's targeted group.

How does a professional get a copy of the competitors' mailings? There are several approaches. Ask a competitor that you may know. Older professionals may be flattered and give a sample to the professional. Another way is to ask the mailing house that provided the mailing list for a sample advertisement. Ask existing clients to gather and tender all direct mailing pieces received from competitors. Many clients gather and keep the mailing pieces until they finally decide which attorney to engage.

b. Length

Determining the right copy length should be a main consideration. The letter should be as long as is needed to accomplish the professional's goal but not a word longer.

An initial gut reaction would suggest that short letters are preferred over long letters because most readers nowadays have short attention spans. Most novices would discourage anything other than a one-page letter believing nobody will read 2-page letters or 4-page letters or more. But direct marketing research suggests that long copy, even very long copy, can outpull shorter letters – in certain situations. So maybe trusting a gut reaction is not always best.

It is not uncommon for homeowners to receive 4-page letters. The marketers are utilizing these mailings and intentionally incurring the extra cost of printing and postage. Nobody thinks those direct mail professionals are misguided or uninformed. Would they do it if the 4-pager is not working? Certainly not. These professionals are pros at tracking and analyzing responses. So, it is established that multi-page direct mail pieces can work.

The issue becomes whether the multi-page mailer is effective for professionals. The answer depends on the professional's goals.

A short one or two-page letter is best when the goal is to generate leads seeking more information. A lead is defined as a request for information that concomitantly provides a prospect's name and contact information. This is the most common form of mailer. It is probably unrealistic to expect a prospect to make one of life's biggest decisions based on a multi-page letter. A consultation request should be anticipated. That is where the deal will be closed, not in the direct mail letter.

A multi-page letter is best when the professional's goal is to generate a prospect who is ready, willing, and able to engage the criminal defense attorney. Criminal defense rights can be complex and require a longer letter. Prospects want to know the price and other facts. The more a professional wants a prospect to pre-qualify themselves, the more information that must be conveyed in the multi-page letter. These prospects want a lot of information before committing to the professional – especially since the price is dramatically higher than normal day-to-day expenditures. The strategy can crater if even one piece of information is missing. An interested prospect will read every word before deciding.

c. Call to Action

Make the "call to action" impossible to miss. State it, repeat it, and repeat it again. The call to action tells the prospect exactly what the professional wants the prospect to do. A professional should direct prospects to contact the professional to schedule a free consultation or to request a free special report. Use A/B testing in parallel direct mail pieces to determine whether the contact should be via phone, email, or web form. Also use A/B testing to determine whether the best offer is a free consultation or free special report – or both. The secret is to offer the prospect something of value in return for the contact information and before asking the prospect to commit to engaging the firm.

Prospects are savvy nowadays. They know the professional will use the contact information to contact them.

It is an implied deal. But that deal benefits the professional. The professional who gives away valuable information is one step closer to filling the sales funnel. Prospects who appreciate the valuable information are one step closer to engaging the attorney. It is a win-win situation.

d. Patience

A professional must be patient when soliciting prospects. Do not try to close the deal prematurely or the deal will crater. That is the reason multi-page letters may be imprudent. Instead, focus on one call to action only. Attention should be on the free consultation or free report. If a lawyer, avoid talking about criminal law, criminal law process, or criminal defense procedures. Save that information for the consultation when the professional is trying to get the prospect to know, like, and trust the lawyer.

The Mailing List

The mailing list is the most important component of a direct mail campaign. The most beautiful marketing piece is a waste of money if it is sent to the wrong people. Imagine a beautiful mailer designed to attract personal injury prospects but it is sent to healthy men who join fitness centers – a waste of limited resources.

a. Types of Mailing Lists

The three major types of mailing lists are the (a) compiled mailing list, (b) response mailing list, and (c) house mailing list. The compiled mailing list is a list of individuals and demographics compiled from proprietary and publicly-available sources, such as telephone listings, voter registrations, self-reported surveys, etc. This type of targeted mailing list usually offers a broad geography and higher volume than other types of mailing lists. A compiled mailing list often is subdivided into categories to make segmenting prospects easier. Lists such as new parents, new movers and homeowners allow a small business to focus on consumers who might meet its target criteria cost-efficiently. This type of mailing list can be particularly useful when a marketer is trying to reach a well-defined segment. For example, a manufacturer of children's educational toys probably will find the use of a new parents list more cost-effective than a general compiled list.

The house mailing list refers to the in-house proprietary customer or subscriber lists of a company or publication. If managed correctly, an in-house mailing list can become increasingly useful.

The response mailing list contains names of individuals who all have responded to a particular offer. These could be buyers, inquirers, subscribers, sweepstakes entrants, or members of a club (i.e., video club, book club). Some professionals prefer response mailing lists because these recipients are the type of people who respond to direct mail marketing campaigns.

b. Mailing List Providers

The professional must obtain the mailing list from a reliable source. Google the phrase "direct mail list providers" and do some due diligence. Ask for a referral from anyone the professional knows who is utilizing direct mail. Contact the American Marketing Association (AMA) and the Data & Marketing Association (DMA). Consider the following six mailing list companies (no recommendation is being made here, just providing information).

- Experian.com

Experian is known for its free consumer credit reports. It also provides direct mail list compiling and management. Experian specializes in maintaining an unfathomable amount of consumer data about all sorts of data points. It is able to leverage its data base to generate highly customizable direct mailing lists that can reach the exact audience a professional is hoping to reach.

- DirectMail.com

DirectMail.com provides direct mailing services and integrated marketing techniques with tools that empower their mailing lists to be as impactful as possible through analytics and data.

- Caldwell-list.com

Caldwell List offers a vast array of parameters for business, consumer, or "specialty" lists. Its staff help identify the best possible mailing list to satisfy the needs of a direct mailing campaign. The ability to order a list based on a mailer's description of the direct mailing campaign's intent is a unique asset that Caldwell List provides not only as a convenience, but as a way of custom fitting the mailing list solution to the list-buyers' budget or geographic needs.

- Listgiant.com

Listgiant's website allows instant access to any of a professional's previously configured counts or orders anytime. Listgiant provides 24/7 portal access to list creation and review tools. This portal replaces the old fashioned but all-too-common source of the list broker. The portal allows the professional to make the most of its lists and it allows for full customization as the professional goes about setting parameters and qualifying leads.

- ProspectsInfluential.com

ProspectsInfluential offers a free in-depth consultation as a professional builds a consumer list from any of its pre-existing list templates or a custom list. ProspectsInfluential list brokers work closely with its clients and provide recommendations and insights into the direct marketing industry.

- ConquestGraphics.com

ConquestGraphics' configurator offers a balance between simplicity and customization, giving the professional the ability to customize the qualifiers that really matter when it comes to forming a direct mail audience.

c. List Brokers

A list broker can be a "captured" broker or an independent broker. A captured broker works for a single mailing list provider as an employee. The captured broker has a duty of loyalty to the mailing list provider and not to the professional.

An independent list broker is different. An independent broker works with multiple mailing list providers. Theoretically, the independent broker selects the mailing list provider that best suits the professional and not the provider that offers the greatest commission. But beware that the independent list broker's duty of loyalty may be with the list provider since it is paid a commission based on a contract between the independent broker and the mailing list provider.

Independent list brokers work on commission and are paid by the list owner – just like a mortgage broker is paid by the mortgage lender and real estate broker is paid by the seller. Brokers are typically paid a flat fee per list or more typically a percentage of the mailing list rental fee. Either way, the professional would not pay the list broker a fee separate from the list rental fee.

What are the characteristics of a good list broker? Trust comes to mind, as well as accurate lists leased at affordable prices. A good list broker should offer all of the following :

- A+ Better Business Bureau Rating.
- 100s of 5-star online review.
- Accurate, up-to-date lists
- Affordable Lists
- Low Minimums
- Expert Marketing Advice
- Superb Customer Service

After conducting appropriate due diligence, make sure to interview the top three list brokers before making a final selection. Remember, the mailing list is the most important component of a direct mail campaign. Mail sent to the wrong target group could prove worthless and squander limited marketing resources. Consider asking these questions before making a final selection of a list broker:

"What type of lists do you sell?"

"How often do you update your lists? At least every 90 days?"

"How accurate are your lists?"

"How much do your lists cost?"

"Do you guarantee the accuracy of your lists?"

"Will you send me a sample list before I place an order?"

"Do you offer design and sending services for direct mailers and email marketing campaigns?"

DIRECT MAIL SAMPLES – BANKRUPTCY CONTEXT

To help illustrate the effectiveness of direct mail, this section focuses on a lawyer who specializes in consumer bankruptcy protection. The lessons taught herein are just as applicable to lawyers who practice in other substantive areas. These lawyers would have to modify the sample letters to reflect the lawyer's substantive practice area.

Direct Mail Sample – Harassing Phone Calls

Debt collectors frequently harass prospective bankruptcy clients employing a commonly used strategy to collect debts. Debt collectors call on the phone and demand payment. Then they call again, and again, and again. If they could, these prospects would pay the debt collectors in full to stop the harassment. But they cannot. Sure, they may pay a little hoping that would satisfy the debt collectors and stop the harassment. But any reprieve is short lived.

The harassment begins again because the debt balances keep building with administrative charges, attorney's fees, late fees, and interest. It is a downward spiral until finally the prospects reach-out to a bankruptcy attorney to stop the harassment.

A direct mail piece can be effective when sent to prospects suffering from harassing phone calls. Consider the following sample letter:

5/15/2X

Jack Jones

9365 S. Pleasant
Chicago, IL 60620

Re: Discover Card Services v. Jack Jones, 21 AR 12345, Circuit Court of Cook County, IL, Judge: Thomas O'Brand

Dear Jack:

Are bill collectors harassing you on the phone? Are you anxious when your phone rings from a caller with an unidentified number? Do you want peace and quiet?

Protection is only a phone call away. My law firm can force the bill collectors to stop calling you. Peace and quiet can be yours if you only contact the firm to get the ball rolling.

I offer a free consultation to inform you of your right to a debt-free, stress-free fresh start in life. You will be treated with dignity and respect. You can enjoy life again free from harassing phone calls.

Free Consultation! Take action to know your options and stop the wage garnishment. Call today at 312-555-5555 to schedule your FREE consultation. I am considered a debt relief agency and provide people with help filing for bankruptcy relief under the Bankruptcy Code. The bankruptcy disclosures can be found on my website at www.LarryLawyer.com/data.

I look forward to helping you.

Sincerely,

Larry Lawyer
Advertising Material

P.S. Let me help you live a happy tomorrow.

Direct Mail Sample – Wage Garnishment

Prospective bankruptcy clients can be suffering from wage garnishments. A garnishment is a judicial procedure that compels an employer to withhold money from a person's paycheck and tender those funds to a judgment creditor designated by a court.

The existence of a garnishment is a red flag that the prospect owes more debts that the prospect cannot afford to pay. It also signals significant debt problems worthy of talking to a bankruptcy attorney. Consider the following sample letter:

5/15/2X

Cindy Sanders
9215 S. Winchester
Chicago, IL 60620

Re: Chase Card Services v. Cindy Sanders, 21 AR 65321, Circuit Court of Cook County, IL, Judge: Barbara Backty

Dear Cindy:

Feel instant relief and peace of mind during this difficult time in your life. I am very friendly, respectful, and helpful. It will be like talking about your problem with a friend.

- ➤ **Guarantee!** Receive a 100% money-back refund if your wage garnishment is not stopped.
- ➤ **Caring, Compassionate & Non-Judgmental Help!** You will feel comfortable and be treated with dignity and respect. I will listen to your concerns, hear what actions you have taken, and explain your legal options in easy-to-understand terms.

> **5 Minutes to Stop the Wage Garnishment!** Feel instant relief and peace of mind by taking 5 minutes to call my office and schedule your free appointment.

Free Consultation! Take action to know your options and stop the wage garnishment. Call today at 312-555-5555 to schedule your FREE consultation. I am considered a debt relief agency and provide people with help filing for bankruptcy relief under the Bankruptcy Code. The bankruptcy disclosures can be found on my website at www.LarryLawyer.com/data.

I look forward to helping you.

Sincerely,

Larry Lawyer
Advertising Material

P.S. Let me help you live a happy tomorrow.

Direct Mail Sample – Bank Account Levy

A bank account levy can be the final straw that prompts a prospective bankruptcy client to contact a bankruptcy lawyer. A bank account levy allows a creditor to legally take funds from the prospect's bank account. When a bank gets notification of this legal action, it will freeze the prospect's account and send the appropriate funds to the prospect's creditor. In turn, that creditor uses the funds to pay down the debt owed by the prospect. Here is a sample letter:

5/15/2X

Paula Prowder
9433 S. Levitt
Chicago, IL 60620

Re: Ford Motor Credit v. Paula Prowder, 21 L 25874, Circuit Court of Cook County, IL, Judge: Charles Johnson

Dear Paula:

Did your bank freeze your bank account and give your hard-earned money to Ford Motor Credit? Do you want to stop that from happening again?

Get the protection you need now. I offer instant relief and peace of mind during this difficult time in your life. I am very friendly, respectful, and helpful. It will be like talking about your problem with a friend.

> **Caring, Compassionate & Non-Judgmental Help!** You will feel comfortable and be treated with dignity and respect. I will listen to your concerns, hear what actions you have taken, and explain your legal options in easy-to-understand terms.
> **5 Minutes to Stop Future Bank Levies!** Feel instant relief and peace of mind by taking 5 minutes to call my office and schedule your free appointment.

Free Consultation! Take action to know your options and stop the future bank levies. Call today at 312-555-5555 to schedule your FREE consultation. I am considered a debt relief agency and provide people with help filing for bankruptcy relief under the Bankruptcy Code. The bankruptcy disclosures can be found on my website at www.LarryLawyer.com/data.

I look forward to helping you.

Sincerely,

Larry Lawyer
Advertising Material

P.S. Let me help you live a happy tomorrow.

Direct Mail Sample – Lawsuit

Lawsuits are a nightmare to prospective bankruptcy clients. Lawyers become callous towards lawsuits because we studied them in law school and work with them in private practice. They become the stock in trade. It is easy for lawyers to become insensitive to the anxiety surrounding lawsuits.

Not true for prospects. A lawsuit introduces anxiety, worry, uncertainty, and dread. First, a lawsuit can be served by a county sheriff knocking on a prospect's door. Image the anxiety felt by the prospect when opening a door and confronting a uniformed officer tendering court papers with the officer's county sheriff squad car in the background. Pretty intimidating. Next, a lawsuit plunges the prospect into an unfamiliar world of law in which everyone else is skilled and trained in law – everyone except the prospect. Deputy sheriffs, lawyers, and judges. The prospect also worries about the cost. Something bad is about to happen because the prospect acknowledges that the debt is owed. But the prospect cannot afford an attorney to defend. Is there any defense?

This is a good time for a bankruptcy lawyer to solicit the prospect. Consider the solicitation letter below:

5/15/2X

Michael Wardmanson
9234 S. Longwood
Chicago, IL 60620

Re: Capital One Bank v. Michael Wardmanson, 21 L 85268, Circuit Court of Cook County, IL, Judge: Harold McDougal

Dear Michael:

Court records indicate that Capital One Bank filed a lawsuit against you for $8,456.

- Do not let a lawsuit judgment take your paycheck, bank account, or home.
- Read our online reviews.
- Visit our website at www.LarryLawyer.com for complete information.
- Eliminate all debt you can, and keep your car and home.
- Larry Lawyer offers payment plans for everyone.
- Evening and Saturday appointments are available.

Make your FREE office appointment online 24/7 at www.Larry Lawyer.com/appointment. Or, call 312-555-5555 for an appointment and say, "I got your lawsuit mailer." I am considered a debt relief agency and provide people with help filing for bankruptcy relief under the Bankruptcy Code. The bankruptcy disclosures can be found on my website at www.LarryLawyer.com/data.

I look forward to helping you.

Sincerely,

Larry Lawyer
Advertising Material

P.S. Let me help you live a happy tomorrow.

Below is a sample of a much longer solicitation letter that appears too text heavy to be effective. It is presented as an example of what not to send:

5/15/2X

Tonya Tolero

9125 S. Damen
Chicago, IL 60620

Lawsuit Information:

Case No.: 21 SC 35874
Amount: $8,452
Plaintiff: Capital One Bank
Judge: Roger Reynolds

Dear Tonya:

A search of public records has revealed that a lawsuit has been filed against you by Capital One Bank. Jackview Law Firm does not represent the plaintiff in that case. In fact, we never represent creditors. We are a group of Illinois licensed consumer law attorneys whose sole purpose is to protect the rights of ordinary consumers like you. It is our passion. It is our mission.

If a judgment is entered, the judgment may be recorded with the county recorder of deeds and becomes a lien on your real estate, if you own real estate. Also, the judgment may result in a wage garnishment if you are employed or having the funds in your bank account seized via a third-party bank attachment.

Time is of the essence!

There are avenues available under both state and federal law to provide you with relief under these circumstances. Our firm is unique in that we employ a diverse team of attorneys focusing in all areas of consumer law including consumer defense, individual and commercial (business) bankruptcy. Our advice will always be based on what is best for you – period. It is our fiduciary responsibility.

Before taking any action, we ask that you spend some time thoroughly researching the many law firms who are providing you with direct mail advertising. When you do, you will notice that Jackview Law Firm is among the highest rated consumer law firms in the entire country with an AVVO Rating of 10 out of 10 – Exceptional – and who employ multiple Super Lawyers. Please download our book "Your Defense to a Pending Lawsuit: A Tactical Guide to Bankruptcy" for FREE on our website at www.LarryLawyer.com (Retail: $39.99) or you may purchase a hardcopy for your library directly from www.Amazon.com.

Please call us at 312-555-5555 within the next 3 days to allow yourself enough time to schedule an appointment with an attorney and to deal with your situation. Honest advice, dedicated and compassionate service, and exceedingly predictable outcomes are what we provide our clients. What we deliver is real and enduring peace of mind.

Sincerely,

Larry Lawyer
Jackview Law Firm, LLP
Advertising Material

P.S. We are considered a debt relief agency and provide people with help filing for bankruptcy relief under the Bankruptcy Code. The bankruptcy disclosures can be found on my website at www.LarryLawyer.com/data.

Direct Mail Sample – Foreclosure

Foreclosure is a scary word. The thought of losing one's home and being evicted into the street can cause nightmares. Prospects on the verge of foreclosure should be considered a target market. Below is a sample solicitation letter:

5/15/2X

Richard Coleford
9125 S. Damen
Chicago, IL 60620

Re: Chase Manhattan Bank v. Richard Coleford, 21 CH 65489, Circuit Court of Cook County, IL, Judge: Roger Reynolds

Dear Richard:

According to public records, the County Sheriff is scheduled to sell your home as auction on December 12, 202X. We can stop this auction from occurring and save your home. We are a local law firm with a primary focus in bankruptcy, foreclosure defense, and short sales. We pride ourselves in helping people keep their homes and getting out of debt. Our firm has been helping people for over XX years and we know how to stop the sale of your home. Do not hesitate to call us. We will sit down with you and go over your situation to determine the best approach. We offer virtual web-based consultations for your convenience.

Make your FREE office appointment online 4/7 at www.Larry Lawyer.com/appointment. Or call 312-555-5555 for an appointment and say, "I got your foreclosure mailer." I am considered a debt relief agency and provide people with help filing for bankruptcy relief under the Bankruptcy Code. The bankruptcy disclosures can be found on my website at www.LarryLawyer.com/data.

I look forward to helping you.

Sincerely,

Larry Lawyer
Advertising Material

P.S. Let me help you live a happy tomorrow.

Direct Mail Sample – Worker's Compensation

Nobody plans to be temporarily disabled because of a work-related injury. But accidents do happen without advance notice. Prospective bankruptcy clients can be suddenly thrust into financial chaos when an accident occurs, and the prospect is no longer able to work. No work – No paycheck.

Worker's compensation only pays of a portion of your lost wages. Worker's compensation also does not pay anything for the pain and suffering caused by the injury. While this may seem unfair, it is part of the trade-off that is the worker's compensation system. The advantage of worker's compensation is that benefits are paid relatively quickly without needing to file a lawsuit or prove that the employer was at fault for causing the injury. The downside is that the prospect cannot get compensated for the full value of the losses.

A prospect may receive temporary total disability (TTD) benefits if he/she cannot work while recovering from a work-related injury or illness, or if the employer cannot give modified light-duty work that accommodates the prospect's physical limitations. The amount of the TTD benefits will be two-thirds of the prospect's pre-injury average weekly wage, up to a maximum amount that changes periodically.

Most bankruptcy prospects were living on the financial precipice before the work accident. After the accident, the financial chaos intensifies. A reduction of income to two-thirds the normal income just will not cover the expenses and pay the bills. Bankruptcy may be the answer.

Consider the following solicitation letter:

5/15/2X

Tommy Tarham
9125 S. Damen
Chicago, IL 60620

Re: Tommy Tarham v. Ajax Cement Services, 21 WC 12345,
Illinois Worker's Compensation Commission

Dear Tommy:

A recent search of the public records indicate that you are a claimant in a worker's compensation case against Ajax Cement Services. **We do not represent Ajax Cement Services**. If you are having bill problems that are beginning to overwhelm you, we can help. To eliminate your debts come in for a **FREE consultation**.

Our law firm has gained a reputation for success in representing people in Chapter 7 and Chapter 13 bankruptcies. Additionally, we have expanded our services to include debt negotiation.

We will use whatever legal remedies are available to secure an honest solution to your financial problems without jeopardizing your home, car, worker's compensation claim, or other valuable assets. At your **FREE consultation**, you will speak to a lawyer directly. Our attorney will discuss your situation and help you to decide what option will work best for you.

DON'T DELAY. YOUR FRESH START IS JUST A PHONE CALL AWAY!

Make your FREE office appointment by calling us at 312-555-5555. I am considered a debt relief agency and provide people with help filing for bankruptcy relief under the Bankruptcy Code. The bankruptcy disclosures can be found on my website at www.LarryLawyer.com/data.

I look forward to helping you.

Sincerely,

Larry Lawyer
Advertising Material

P.S. Let me help you live a happy tomorrow.

Direct Mail Sample – Divorce

Divorce can lead to deep financial chaos, especially when the root cause of the divorce was toxic debt. The divorce may minimize fighting between the now ex-spouses, but the divorce does not solve the debt problems.

Two incomes were insufficient to pay the bills while married. Now the increased costs associated with maintaining two separate households exacerbate the financial chaos.

Bankruptcy can be the answer to eliminate the unmanageable debt. Divorced people should be receptive to the possibility of a debt-free fresh start in life. Below is a sample solicitation letter:

5/15/2X

Diane McMillan
9411 S. Hoyne
Chicago, IL 60620

Re: Diane McMillan v. Leonard McMillan, 21 D 96358, Circuit Court of Cook County, IL, Judge: Benjamin Brown

Dear Diane:

Has divorce left you struggling with debts you cannot afford to pay? Would you like a debt-free, stress-free fresh start in life?

We offer instant relief and peace of mind during this difficult time in your life. Let us guide you to financial independence from bill collectors, harassing phone calls, lawsuits, and wage garnishments.

I am very friendly, respectful, and helpful. It will be like talking about your problem with a friend.

> **Caring, Compassionate & Non-Judgmental Help!** You will feel comfortable and be treated with dignity and respect. I will listen to your concerns, hear what actions you have taken, and explain your legal options in easy-to-understand terms.
> **5 Minutes to Stop Creditors!** Feel instant relief and peace of mind by taking 5 minutes to call my office and schedule your free appointment.

Free Consultation! Take action to know your options and stop bill collectors, harassing phone calls, lawsuits, and wage garnishments. Call today at 312-555-5555 to schedule your FREE consultation. We are considered a debt relief agency and provide people with help filing for bankruptcy relief under the Bankruptcy Code. The bankruptcy disclosures can be found on my website at www.LarryLawyer.com/data.

I look forward to helping you.

Sincerely,

P.S. Let me help you live a happy tomorrow.

CONTACT PROSPECTS FOLLOWING FREE CONSULTATION

Assume a prospective bankruptcy client accepts the free consultation offer and meets with the attorney. Hopefully that prospect engages the bankruptcy attorney at the conclusion of the consultation. But what should the lawyer do if the prospect is indecisive and says,

"I need to think about what you said and talk it over with my wife. I will get back to you in a couple days."

The answer is sequential follow-up direct mail marketing. A lawyer should have pre-planned direct mail marketing pieces ready to be dripped-out over a period of months. Bankruptcy prospects are known for burying their heads in the sand hoping for disaster to go away through inaction. Only occasionally do those prospects remove their head from the sand and take action. When that will be is a case-by-case determination. The lawyer should try to be visible when the magical moment comes, and the prospect is ready to act.

A good direct mail marketing sequence is as follows:

- Letter 1: mailed 7 days after the consultation.
- Letter 2: mailed 14 days after the consultation.
- Letter 3: mailed 30 days after the consultation.
- Letter 4: mailed 60 days after the consultation
- Letter 5: mailed 90 days after the consultation.

A typical bankruptcy prospect does not like meeting with a lawyer because it can be an intimidating experience. A caring, compassionate, and non-judgmental approach must be employed during the consultation. Displaying empathy is the key.

The tendency to procrastinate is probably the reason a prospect fails to engage an empathetic lawyer, all other things being equal. So, the engagement is just a matter of time.

Lawyers should understand that the money comes from the follow-up direct mail marketing campaign. Below are sample letters 1-5.

Letter 1 Mailed 7 Days Post-Consultation

5/15/2X

Brian Moynahan
9223 S. Damen
Chicago, IL 60620

Re: Chase Manhattan Bank v. Moynahan, 21 L 25836, Circuit Court of Cook County, IL, Judge: Robert McKenert

Dear Brian:

Thank you for meeting with me last week to discuss solutions to your financial crisis. I hope the information we gave you was useful. Debt problems do not go away by themselves. In fact, debt problems only get worse without taking action.

A debt-free life can begin today!

Image how you will feel with a fresh start in life that is debt-free, stress-free, and worry-free.

I have enclosed another copy of the engagement letter for you to sign and return to me. I cannot begin to help you until you return the signed documents with your retainer payment of $1,995.

Act today! Do not put off solving your financial problems any longer.

Please call me if you have further questions or if you want to make another appointment with me to sign the papers in person at my office.

I look forward to helping you.

Sincerely,

Larry Lawyer

P.S. The sooner we receive the engagement letter and retainer the sooner we can help you.

Letter 2 Mailed 14 Days Post-Consultation

5/15/2X

Brian Moynahan
9223 S. Damen
Chicago, IL 60620

Re: Chase Manhattan Bank v. Moynahan, 21 L 25836, Circuit Court of Cook County, IL, Judge: Robert McKenert

Dear Brian:

HAVE THE BILL COLLECTORS BEEN HARASSING YOU OVER THE PAST 14 DAYS SINCE WE LAST MET?

You do not have to be afraid anymore. We can solve your financial problems. We have helped hundreds of other people just like you and we want to help you too.

A debt-free life can begin today!

Here is what one of my clients said about seeking help:

- I suffered unnecessarily by procrastinating.
- I wished I had taken action right away.
- My life has completely changed for the better.
- I enjoy a fresh start in life that is debt-free, stress-free, and worry-free.

Why are you waiting to take action to help yourself? Act today! Do not put off solving your financial problems any longer.

Please call me if you have further questions or if you want to make another appointment with me to sign the papers in person at my office.

I look forward to helping you.

Sincerely,

Larry Lawyer

P.S. The sooner we receive the engagement letter and retainer the sooner we can help you.

Letter 3 Mailed 30 Days Post-Consultation

5/15/2X

Brian Moynahan
9223 S. Damen
Chicago, IL 60620

Re: Chase Manhattan Bank v. Moynahan, 21 L 25836, Circuit Court of Cook County, IL, Judge: Robert McKenert

Dear Brian:

You have let a month slip away without taking any action. Answer these questions truthfully:

- Has the financial chaos gone away or intensified?
- Are you still getting harassing phone calls?
- Are you fighting with your spouse over money problems?

I would be delighted to meet with you again to answer any questions that you still have. Do not worry about being charged for more attorney time. I extend an offer for an additional consultation FREE OF CHARGE.

Alternatively, you can sign and return the enclosed engagement letter with your retainer deposit. Don't have the money saved right now? No worries. We can work out a payment arrangement that meets your budget.

Let's make today the day you take action to start a debt-free life. I am ready to help.

Sincerely,

Larry Lawyer

P.S. Let us eliminate your worries. We are only a phone call away!

Letter 4 Mailed 60 Days Post-Consultation

5/15/2X

Brian Moynahan
9223 S. Damen
Chicago, IL 60620

Re: Chase Manhattan Bank v. Moynahan, 21 L 25836, Circuit Court of Cook County, IL, Judge: Robert McKenert

Dear Brian:

Solutions were offered 60 days ago. But you still have not taken action. Isn't now the time to act?

Financial problems have a way of depressing a person and creeping into all aspects of your life. Are you losing sleep or lying awake in bed worrying about the chaos?

We understand that stress and worry can be overwhelming. That is why we want to help you today. We have helped hundreds of other people just like you.

Image how you would feel if your financial crisis disappeared overnight? What would be the first thing you do after reaching financial freedom?

We know how to eliminate your creditors. Please call to schedule your next appointment or send in your signed engagement letter today with the deposit.

A debt-free life is just around the corner if you let us help you!

Sincerely,

Larry Lawyer

P.S. Stop your financial nightmares today.

Letter 5 Mailed 90 Days Post-Consultation

5/15/2X

Brian Moynahan
9223 S. Damen
Chicago, IL 60620

Re: Chase Manhattan Bank v. Moynahan, 21 L 25836, Circuit Court of Cook County, IL, Judge: Robert McKenert

Dear Brian:

LAST CHANCE!

It has been 90 days since we met in my office. I explained how we can eliminate your debts and offered you a fresh start in life again. This is the last letter to you before we close our file and move on to help other clients get a fresh start.

We have sent you multiple letters urging you to act. We are flexible and can offer another free consultation or offer a payment plan within your budget if that is holding you back.

Remember, your financial crisis will only deepen without action. The problems typically will not go away without professional help and action. The attorney's fees, late fees, and interest are only going to compound without action.

Again, this is our last letter to you. We want to help but we have to hear from you. **A debt-free life can begin today!**

Sincerely,

Larry Lawyer

P.S. We will close the file and move on to help other people if we do not hear from you within 5 days.

Final Note

Direct mail marketing can be an effective tool in a lawyer's advertising toolbox. But it should not be the only tool. The best marketing plans cross-pollinate with referral marketing, direct mail marketing, email marketing, website marketing, social media marketing, and more.

SECRET 10: BROCHURE MARKETING

Brochure marketing is still viable and has not been obliterated by digital marketing as some experts claim. In fact, brochure marketing should be used in conjunction with digital marketing to maximize impact.

Brochures are one of the most effective and versatile marketing tools used to inform prospective clients of the professional's services. They are simple to produce compared to other forms of marketing. Brochures are cost effective and easy to distribute. Brochure marketing is well worth adding to a professional's marketing toolbox.

A custom brochure is a marketing staple that gives a professional extra room to tell a story, present prospects with services, or simply promote sales. Compact and versatile, professional brochures can be distributed at events, sent as mailing inserts, or placed on office countertops.

The three-panel, tri-fold brochure also allows a professional to communicate a marketing message without being present. Brochures project a brief, but informative version of the professional's advertising message. Brochures can:

- Relay core ideas
- Introduce new services
- Explain existing services
- And much more.

Goal of Brochure Marketing

The #1 goal of brochure marketing is to compel a prospective client to contact the professional! Once contact, the door is open for the professional to close the deal by convincing the prospect to engage the attorney.

10 Benefits of Brochure Marketing

Here are the top 10 benefits of utilizing brochure marketing to attract prospects:

1. **Gets the prospect to contact the professional.** The prospect must make the first move.

2. **Positions the professional as an expert.** A brochure can describe the professional's abilities and identify how the professional can help the prospect. A brochure helps a prospect view the professional as an expert.

3. **Testimonials prove the point.** Prospects will put themselves in the shoes of the professional's past clients who have benefitted from the attorney's services. Testimonials are an implied endorsement of the professional's skills. Two to three testimonials should be included in a brochure. Add client pictures with their permission.

4. **Enhances the professional's credibility.** A professionally designed and printed brochure indicates to prospects that the professional is a true professional qualified to solve the prospects' crises.

5. **Portability increases impact.** Brochures are portable and can be taken wherever prospects travel. Desktop digital marketing is limited by the length of the monitor cord. Cell phone digital marketing is limited by the size of the screen and frequency of a social media advertisement. A brochure can be stuffed into a woman's purse or man's pocket for later study.

6. **Reading when ready**. Remember that prospects can be procrastinators. They act when they are ready to act and not a moment earlier. Having a brochure in a person's purse or pocket is easily assessable when a prospect has the urge to act. A digital ad may hit a prospect at the wrong time. The brochure sits in a prospect's possession until the magical moment. Also, brochure marketing allows a prospect the time to study what services the professional offers and what solutions the professional can provide.

7. **Retention is key**. Prospects will save a brochure – sometimes for months. A prospect will not throw away a brochure that offers the very solution they need and identifies the very person who can provide that solution. No. A prospect will retain the brochure until his/her head is pulled out of the sand and the prospect decides to act.

8. **Cost effective marketing tool**. Brochures are far less expense than digital advertising, newspaper advertising, TV advertising, and many other forms of advertising. The bang for the buck is best when used in conjunction with other forms of advertising.

9. **Proven track record**. Brochures are ubiquitous because they are effective. Brochures seem to be everywhere a person goes. They can be found in professional offices of lawyers, accountants, doctors, dentists, and architects. Labor providers use them like plumbers, electricians, and roofers. Bulletin boards are covered with them at food stores, community centers, and laundry mats.

10. **Success is around the corner**. A prospect that retains a professional's brochure will probably call the

professional at some point after reading the brochure. The timing is uncertain, but the call will most likely happen. After all, that is the #1 goal – getting the prospect to call the professional.

Cost of Brochure Marketing

Brochures may be one of the least expensive marketing strategies a professional can use to disseminate information. The industry standard is tri-folded, 8.5 x 11-inch, glossy or matte paper, printed on both sides. The per-piece cost varies with the quantity ordered. The larger the quantity, the lower the cost because most of the cost relates to the printing setup charges. For example, www.vistaprint.com is offering the industry standard brochures at the following cost:

Quantity	Total Cost	Per Piece Cost
10,000	$762.23	$0.076
5,000	$460.63	$0.092
2,500	$306.93	$0.122
1,000	$206.38	$0.206
250	$124.29	$0.497

Quantity

Order 5,000 for the first run. The cost per the chart above would be a little over 9¢ each. That is a bargain for the marketing power a brochure generates.

Some professionals may worry that 5,000 is more than a professional can realistically use. Not so if used correctly. A professional should flood the market with brochures, distributing them throughout the community. As explained later below, a professional should distribute brochures everywhere prospective clients may roam and everywhere referring sources may be.

Quality

Always have brochures printed professionally. Some professionals may utilize colored printers in their office offices. Do not use them for marketing. It would be a mistake. The quality of professional printers is vastly superior to anything most professionals would own.

Some professional printers offer brochures printed on fancier paper than the industry standard and offer them at a premium price. The extra money may not be worth it. The quality of the professional printed industry standard paper should be high enough quality for most consumer markets.

Before placing an order, contact the printer and ask the printer to send a few samples of brochures printed for other customers. Inspect the quality carefully. Most professional printers should provide an excellent product.

Distributees

A professional's entire community should receive a brochure – everyone within the professional's contact sphere. Brochures should be distributed to anyone who contacts the firm. Every caller gets a brochure. Every consultation should start or end with handing a brochure to the prospect. Every direct mail piece should include a letter and brochure.

Display brochures at public locations like gas stations, food stores, community centers, and coffee houses. A great place to display brochures is at a pawnshop because people pawning valuables are probably in deep debt.

Distribute brochures at the next bar association meeting or Rotary club meeting. Offer to speak at a local chamber of commerce lunch meeting and place a brochure on each plate.

A top choice is to ask all strategic partners to display the brochures in their professional offices. Some professionals run behind schedule and some clients/patients/customers arrive prior to scheduled appointments. Consequently, a waiting room or reception area is a perfect place to have a stack of brochures because the clients/patients/customers are waiting with nothing else to do except read the brochure. Make reciprocal arrangements with these strategic partners and offer to display their brochures in the professional's office.

Display brochures at the following offices:

- Divorce attorneys
- CPAs, bookkeepers, and tax preparers
- Worker's compensation attorneys
- Marriage counselors
- Credit counselors
- Distressed Car dealers
- Mortgage brokers
- Realtors

10 Design Issues

Designing a marketing brochure has never been so easy. In the old days, professionals had to hire graphic designers to professional design a brochure at the cost of hundreds and hundreds of dollars. Today, most online printers offer designing for free. The online printers offer web-based graphic design dashboards that allow professionals to custom design brochures at no extra cost.

Here are the top 10 issues that must be considered when designing a professional's brochure:

1. **Remember the goal.** The #1 goal of brochure marketing is to compel a prospective client to contact the professional! Leave the curriculum vitae for another day.

2. **A strong headline grabs attention.** The top of a brochure must grab the prospect's attention within two seconds. The best headline contains five words are less. Consider the phrase, "Got Debt?" These two little words create a punch that appeals to anyone with toxic debt or suffering with financial chaos.

3. **Pictures are worth a thousand words.** It is an old adage meaning that complex ideas can be conveyed by a single image. This adage is never truer than in brochure marketing because space is limited to two sides of an 8.5 x 11-inch paper. So, whose picture(s) should be displayed? The best brochures contain multiple pictures, including the professional's picture above the professional's brief bio and two pictures of past clients above their testimonials.

4. **Focus on the phone number.** The professional's phone number is fundamental and must be accessible. The purpose of the brochure is to get the prospect to call the professional. So, make it easy on the prospect. Place the phone number on the front page near the bottom, on the last page near the bottom, and in at least one of the inside panels. A prospect may not read the entire brochure. The prospect may decide to call the professional after reading only part of the brochure. Do not make the prospect hunt for the phone number.

5. **Email is mandatory**. Gone are the days when professionals only used phones and maybe faxes. The modern professional has to be accessible by email and offer it as a communications option for prospects. If the prospect would rather email then call, then make it easy for the prospect. It is the prospect's choice.

6. **Web forms are great**. Another strong electronic communication option is the web-based contact form on the "Contact Us" page of the professional's website. The contact form has required fields for the prospect's name, phone, email, and problems needing solutions. Clients who are computer literate can be better clients because communicating electronically may be easier. Low-tech clients should be avoided.

7. **Hit 3 unique selling points ("USP")**. Explain why the professional should be contacted by the prospect instead of the professional's competitors. A USP must be fundamental to the professional's practice and not just an empty slogan. A USP must concisely communicate that the prospect's needs will be met. Plus, a USP must punctuate a difference between the professional and competitors. What does the professional offer than competitors do not?

8. **Testimonials are tremendous**. Testimonials are written statements that support the professional's credibility and underscore the professional's level of expertise. Prospects want to know what will happen to them if they choose the professional. Testimonials speak to that desire. A prospect is able to stand in the shoes of a professional's client via a testimonial. They are powerful, so include at least two testimonials. Use the testimonials that most closely reflect the professional's targeted demographic.

9. **No legalese**. Save the legal terminology and legal jargon for the bar association meetings. Do not use "fractured distal radius" when debt "broken wrist" is easier to understand. Use plain and simple language that a professional would use talking to the professional's mother. A lawyer should not say, "the defendant's negligence was the proximate cause of the insured event." No, a lawyer talking to his/her mother would say, "the other driver rammed his car into my client's car causing a broken wrist."

10. **Call the prospect to action**. Give clear direction what the professional wants the prospect to do. The "call-to-action" is a phrase that is used to tell the prospect exactly what action to take and how to take it. It can be as simple as two word – "Call Now!" or "Call for a Free Consultation."

Ok, you were promised the top 10 issues that must be considered when designing a professional's brochure. Here is a bonus issue.

11. **End with an offer**. A professional has to give to receive. Provide an irresistible offer to prompt the prospect to contact the professional. The most common offer is a free consultation. However, this offer is so common that it has lost its punch. A free "special report," on the other hand, may pique the prospects interest and motivate the prospect to call. A professional who desires more technologically sophisticated clients should offer a "special report" that is downloadable via the professional's website through a web form. The web form captures the prospect's contact information including name, email address, and phone number. The special report is the perfect topic to discuss when the professional contacts

The Rainmaker's 17 Secrets to Marketing & Advertising

the prospect. So, make the special report something that directly affects people who are financial distress. Consider a title like, "5-Steps to Financial Freedom and a Fresh Start in Life."

SECRET 11: NEWSLETTER MARKETING

C linically speaking, newsletter marketing is the strategy by which professionals send informational and service-focused content via U.S. mail or email to a subscriber base that compromises prospective and existing clients. Newsletter marketing is the younger sister of direct mail marketing. Newsletters are really a subset of direct mail letters, but a special chapter is warranted because of the effectiveness of newsletters in certain arenas.

Paper vs. Email

Newsletter marketing involves sending out informational newsletters to interested parties via the U.S. Postal Service. Newsletter marketing, as used here, is distinguished from "email marketing," which is discussed elsewhere.

Marketing Plan

Every successful plan begins with a specific goal. Knowing the goal helps a professional structure the newsletter and tailor it to the targeted recipients. **A professional's primary purpose in distributing newsletters should be maximizing profits by increasing the number of prospect referrals.** A professional must define (a) the target market who will receive the newsletters, and (b) the purpose for sending the newsletters.

The target market for distribution consists of three subparts: (1) current clients; (2) former clients; and (3) prospective clients. Professionals should distribute newsletters to current and former clients. Professionals should not expend limited marketing resources on sending newsletters to prospective clients (send them direct mail instead).

Professionals should expect newsletters to be indirectly distributed to prospective clients by existing or former clients. Do not be surprised when a newsletter is tendered by a current or former client to a prospective client who is a friend or family member.

Newsletters are sent to current and former clients to remind them of the superior service provided by the professional. These clients are the professional's biggest fans already. Periodic newsletters serve as continued reminders. Without them, past clients can forget about the professional and therefore fail to serve as an active referral source.

Newsletters keep the professional in the forefront of the past clients' thoughts. Expect a high-quality newsletter to be retained by current and past clients with a long shelf life. Clients place newsletters on kitchen counters, tabletops, and in drawers. People do not subscribe to newspapers and magazines at the same rate as they used to. As a result, newsletters could be displayed by a table lamp as magazines used to be. That would be a perfect place for the newsletter to be seen by a visiting family member or friend.

Finally, knowing the purpose of the newsletter helps the professional set goals for the campaign. These goals might include increasing referrals by 20%, or increasing revenues by 10%. The professional can then track the results as part of data analytics.

Size & Length

Newsletters should be professionally printed on paper that is 17 inches wide and 11 inches long. Fold the newsletter vertically along the y-axis to create 4 separate panels, each 8 ½ x 11 inches. Then fold the newsletter horizontally along the x-axis for mailing purposes. The address block and postage go on one side of the outer surface. The main header appears on the other side of the outer surface.

Four separate panels represent the perfect size. Enough space to provide interesting content, but not too long that the professional struggles to fill the content. Readers do not want to be bogged down with endlessly long newsletters. Doing less can make a bigger impact.

Distribution Frequency

Newsletters should be sent monthly without interruption. Frequency and consistency are important. A professional must remain in the forefront of the minds of current and past clients. The professional never knows when a referral opportunity will pop up. Therefore, constant reminders are important. Imagine sending a newsletter every 90 days but a referral opportunity arises 80 days after the last newsletter. A friend asks the professional's former client who represented the client, but the former client cannot remember and did not save the last newsletter. The result is a missed opportunity and lost profit. The professional saved $1 each month by not sending that former client a newsletter every month, but lost $1,995 in potential revenue.

Content

Newsletters must be interesting! They are not mini law review articles. Start the newsletter journey by reading the competitors' newsletters to see what kinds of articles they are offering.

Newsletter content should contain a range of ideas to keep the reader interested. Professionals are used to reading long, detailed material. Clients are not. Content ideas include:

- Testimonials

- How-to's
- Problems/Solutions
- Opinion/Analysis
- Reviews
- Best of lists
- Horror/Disaster stories
- Interviews
- Quizzes
- Funny or inspiring anecdotes
- Links
- Event reminders
- Surveys
- Case Studies
- Looks into the future
- Helpful tips

Now for the secret sauce. A "call-to-action" must be strategically placed throughout the newsletter. It cannot be obvious or the client will stop reading. A maximum of 20% of the newsletter should be devoted to the professional's call to action. The remainder should be fun or interesting to the reader.

Remember, the goal of the professional's newsletter marking campaign: **maximizing profits by increasing the number of prospect referrals.** Therefore, the call to action is referring friends, family, and contacts to the professional for services. So, the professional must stealthily weave the call to action into the newsletter. The newsletter sounds like an advertisement if more than 20% of the content is the call to action.

Testimonials

Testimonials are perfect material to weave the call to action. Imagine the impact of the following testimonial:

"I did not know which attorney to contact so I asked my friend Janet the name of the attorney she used to write her last will and testament. I was so happy Janet shared her knowledge with me. I just wish Janet had told me sooner, so I did not have to suffer as much as I did. Thank God for friends!"

This stealthy testimonial emphasizes the call to action (referral of a friend) and highlights how thankful the friend was for the referral. This type of testimonial would encourage and motivate a current or former client to refer friends, family, and contacts.

Celebrities

Every newsletter should contain a segment about celebrities who filed bankruptcy. Clients love reading about famous people who had to go through the same bankruptcy process as the clients. Misery loves company apparently. Just Google "famous people who filed bankruptcy" and receive "about 2,340,000 results." According to Google, famous people who filed bankruptcy include:

- Abraham Lincoln
- Ulysses S. Grant
- Thomas Jefferson
- Walt Disney
- Dave Ramsey
- Larry King
- Randy Quaid
- Willie Nelson
- Burt Reynolds

- Wayne Newton
- Meatloaf
- Mickey Rooney
- Lynn Redgrave
- Toni Braxton
- MC Hammer
- George Jones
- Jerry Lewis
- Margot Kidder
- Anita Bryant
- Marvin Gaye
- David Bowie
- Mick Fleetwood
- Isaac Hayes
- Milton Hershey
- Ronald Isley
- P.T. Barnum
- John Connally
- Mickey Rooney
- Bjorn Borg
- Gary Busey
- Terrell Owens
- Stephen Baldwin
- Jose Conseco
- Archie Griffin
- Merle Haggard
- Perez Hilton
- Don Johnson
- Zsa Gabor
- Natalie Cole
- Tammy Wynette
- David Crosby
- Jackie Mason

- Cindy Lauper
- Pat Paulson
- George McGovern
- Red Foxx
- Latoya Jackson
- Bowie Kuhn
- Francis Ford Coppola
- Gary Coleman
- Kim Basinger
- Peter Bogdonovitch
- Melvin Belli
- Dorothy Hamill
- Johnny Unitas
- Lawrence Taylor
- Leon Spinks
- Gaylord Perry
- Mark Twain
- Oscar Wilde
- Henry Ford
- J.C. Penney
- Nicholas Cage
- Mike Tyson
- Joe Lewis
- Warran Sap
- Vince Neil

SECRET 12: EMAIL MARKETING

Email is ubiquitous. Virtually everyone has access to email in the modern day. Attorneys should decline representing prospects who do not have email access. Without email, it is harder for the attorney to tender documents and pleadings, it is harder to prove instructions and directions were give, it is harder to remind clients of their duties (i.e., attend the § 341 meeting of creditors), it is harder to send confirming emails. The lack of email access is a red flag that trouble is ahead. Expect an ethics complaint at some point with a client alleging lack of communication. Just do not accept a prospect who does not have email access.

Email marketing focuses on a professional's subscriber base that includes prospective clients, current clients, and former clients. Email marketing is a blend of newsletter marketing and direct mail marketing with an electronic twist. All entail disseminating information to interested parties but only email marketing is electronic. Some professionals elect to send newsletters and direct mail via the U.S. Postal Service. However, the vast majority of professionals today connect with their subscriber base via email **only**. Professionals should resist the trend and use **both** email and paper delivered via U.S. mail.

Marketing professional services via email can be fast, flexible, and cost-effective method of reaching prospects and retaining existing clients by encouraging repeat visits to a professional's website. Email marketing allows a professional to create personalized messages to the professional's targeted audience. Emails can incorporate links to specialized landing pages to improve response rates to an email marketing campaign. As a limitation, emails can irritate prospects and clients if they are irrelevant, too frequent, or unwanted. Email

167

marketing can be overused. A discussion of the advantages and disadvantages is below.

Advantages of Email Marketing

Many of the benefits of email marketing to a professional's subscriber base are obvious. First, email marketing is cost-effective. The cost of email marketing can be much lower than many competing forms of marketing. There is no expense for printing, advertising, or media space. Best of all, email newsletters are free to deliver.

Second, subscriber-based emails are, by definition, only sent to people who have actively chosen to receive email communications from the professional. Prospects and clients who are genuinely interest in the professional's service are more likely to engage with the professional and refer prospective clients.

Third, email marketing offers the beauty of flexible design. Emails can be plain text, text with graphics, or text with graphics and attached files. Many graphics are free to download from the internet and insert into an email. Attached files can be a "special report" or an interesting "How To ..." article leading to additional referrals.

Email marketing allows a professional to scale a campaign to reach a large audience or a small, targeted list. A professional can segment a subscriber base into smaller components and tailor different emails to appeal to each of the segments. Consequently, the recipients will receive messages that they are most interested in, helping boost engagement with the professional.

Email marketing is perfect for personalization. No generic "To Whom it May Concern." Email marketers incorporate a recipient's name, address, and other personal information into each email. Personalized emails appear to be emails written by the attorney just for the recipient, without expending the corresponding time.

Shareability is essential to build referrals. Emails are easy to forward to friends, family, and a recipient's contact list. Every time a person shares an email it builds the professional's reputation and expands the professional's referral pool.

Email marketing allows professionals to connect with the subscriber base in real time. Using automated triggers, such as website activity, form completion, subscriptions, professionals can reach a targeted audience with the right message at the right time.

Email marketing empowers attorneys to test alternative email designs and measure results. Professionals can use A/B testing of subject lines, calls-to-action, personalization, text, images, and attachments to maximize marketing effectiveness. Tinkering with these issues can help create the "perfect" email marketing campaign. Using web analytics software, professionals can evaluate the success of a campaign.

Disadvantages of Email Marketing

There are fewer disadvantages than advantages, but the disadvantages are significant and must be addressed. First, spam is a huge problem for email marketers. Emails that appear to be spam irritate prospects and clients. Segmenting and message relevancy is critical to avoid the spam tag. If the emails are not targeted correctly, the recipient may delete the email or worse – unsubscribe from the professional's subscriber base. The "open" rate of emails perceived as spam is nil.

Undelivered emails are another disadvantage. Subscriber data bases must be monitored, and email addresses updated to stay accurate. If a client changes email addresses, then that change must be reflected in the database. A poorly drafted email may not get delivered even if the email address is accurate because internet service providers (ISPs) use software to automatically filter emails that appear to be spam. ISPs' software look for the following terms: FREE, click here, Buy Now, etc. Emails with those words in the subject header could be deleted or stuffed automatically into recipients' spam folders. Many recipients may never look in their spam folders while others do not even know they have spam folders.

File size is another disadvantage of an email marketing campaign directed at working-class prospects and clients. Many of these people own older computers that have insufficient random-access memory (RAM) to open and process emails with large file sizes. An email's file size increases when images, graphics, and attachments are added to a text email. Email marketers must recognize that prospects and clients suffering financial troubles do not have sufficient funds to buy new computers with larger RAM. Instead, they keep their computers until they cease to function. The email file size must be small enough to download quickly. An email containing images and attachments may not download at all or download so slowly that the recipient gets frustrated and just deletes the email without reading it. Professionals must find the optimal balance between an easy to open, text-only email and a harder to open, but more impactful, text with image(s) email.

SECRET 13: NEWSPAPER MARKETING

Newspaper advertising can play an integral role in client development. Many professionals who join a chamber of commerce or service club are local businesspeople who want to market themselves to a local community. Advertising in the local newspaper can do just that. Make the local newspaper editor your best friend!

Many communities enjoy a local paper and read it with regularity. Local papers highlight local news, doings, education, children's sports, etc. Local papers are a credible source of information on local issues. Advertising in the local paper is a great way to build a consistent reliable relationship with a neighborhood audience. The paper's creditability is transferred to the professional.

Realtors, bankers, financial planners, lawyers, accountants, and other professionals should consider branding themselves and their services with regular and consistent advertising. Become the "go to" person in the community with a display ad or insert.

A display ad is the more traditional type of ad. Display ads are found inside the newspaper next to articles. Professionals can choose a range of sizes and where the professional would like it located inside the paper. Be sure to include a "head-shot" picture so the professional can be easily identified and associated with the service provided.

An insert ad is different from a display ad. An insert ad is typically larger than a display ad and could be a full-page ad that stands alone within the newspaper. An insert might work best if the professional has more pictures or information that takes more room than a traditional display ad.

Many advertising experts believe frequency and not size is the most potent formula for professional advertising. A weekly display ad can run for many weeks before the cost equals the cost of a single display ad. Frequency and repetition win the day. A single insert shot can be a waste limited advertising resources and should be avoided.

A display ad needs to make a great first impression. A professional's picture and an eye-catching headline make or break the ad. Prospective clients will move on to the next article or page. Take some time to create a short, impactful headline that leads with the most enticing benefit.

A dynamic display must be clean and simple. Readers have short attention spans nowadays thanks to social media. If the ad is hard to read or confusing, then the reader skips the ad. Keep the ad limited to two fonts and ensure there is plenty of white space around the text. Finally, a display ad should have a clear call-to-action. Tell the reader what should be done after reading the ad.

Most professionals would be better served by avoiding the large city newspaper – in which an advertisement could get lost amid relentless ad clutter. Professionals whose prospective client pool is a local community should not waste money on prospects who would never consider engaging the professional because of geographical undesirability.

SECRET 14: LINKEDIN MARKETING

L inkedIn is America's leading online networking platform designed exclusively for professionals. LinkedIn hosts about 690 million users. Every attorney should be embracing LinkedIn and harnessing the benefits of online professional networking.

LinkedIn is different from a firm website. A firm website showcases a professional's field of expertise, urges prospects to contact the firm, and – with better websites – offers a unique value proposition that differentiates the firm from other firms. Only tangentially does a web site shares information about the professionals working for the firm. Sure, there is typically an "About Us" page but it is not the thrust of the firm website model.

In contrast, LinkedIn showcases a professional's professional profile. The professional is the central focus, not the firm. LinkedIn allows a professional to expand a marketing network by sharing the professional's current job, professional experience, education, volunteer experience, licenses, certificates, publications, honors, awards, organizations, and more.

Why use LinkedIn? First and foremost, LinkedIn is a networking tool for professionals. Professionals can seek connections with other professionals to facilitate cross referrals. Professionals can even find strategic marketing partners through LinkedIn. LinkedIn also helps professionals to be found when prospective clients conduct LinkedIn searches by name. Brand building is important to professionals and LinkedIn helps attorneys build their brands, so they stand out in the bar and demonstrate their marketability. LinkedIn should be used by attorneys to build their reputations and attract prospective clients. LinkedIn also serves as a job board and helps professionals recruit associates as their firms expand. LinkedIn also helps professionals find employment opportunities.

What are some of LinkedIn best practices? Just keep reading.

"Picture" Section - First Impressions

You only get one chance to make a first impression. That adage is applicable to LinkedIn. A professional should spend time polishing the professional's profile page. As an example of a profile page, see the author's profile page at https://www.linkedin.com /in/robert-schaller.

The professional's picture is the first think a visitor sees on a professional's profile page. People form a first impression in a nanosecond of seeing the picture. So, make it nice. A professional should upload a picture taken by a professional photographer and not just a self-pic. A professional should be smiling because studies show people warm to strangers who are smiling faster than strangers who are not smiling. Every LinkedIn profile page has a space for a professional's picture. The default is a grey circle with a stick-figure picture icon as the default should a professional fail to upload a picture. Never forget to upload a picture when creating a profile page.

Professional dress is mandatory. LinkedIn is not a social media site for sharing beach pictures from a spring-break vacation. Use Facebook, Instagram, or Snapchat for that. LinkedIn is all about projecting professionalism and networking. A controversy exists as to what part of the professional's body should be shown in the picture. Some commentators believe that the best picture is a headshot with only the bare minimum of clothing revealed – like the top of a suit jacket or dress. Other commentators suggest a head to mid-chest picture is better. Almost no commentators assert that a full body picture is best because the LinkedIn picture size is limited to a circle with a two-inch diameter. The professional's head would be about the size of a corn kernel when a full body picture is uploaded.

A second picture should be uploaded to the professional's profile page. That photo represents the page banner at the top of the profile page. The professional's profile picture appears half in the banner and half below the banner on the far left-hand side. The default banner is subject to change by LinkedIn and can appear to be aqua blue with geometric shapes. A professional who uses the default banner is not projecting the desired professional look and will find it difficult to connect with other professionals. The banner photo should be used to send a message to fellow professionals who will be considering "connecting" with the professional. Some professionals want to convey a message of credibility by uploading a picture of educational degrees, law licenses, and certificates earned. Other professionals want to convey a message indicating the benefits a fellow professional can achieve by connecting with the professional. Remember, the thrust of LinkedIn is networking by connecting with other professionals.

"Headline" Section

After the pictures, the "headline" is the next most important feature on a professional's profile page, which appears just below the professional's name. A professional's headline describes a professional's expertise in a very limited number of characters (about 219 characters including spaces, which is less than twitter's 280-character limit). This brief description appears next to the professional's name in search results conducted by fellow professionals looking to connect.

The headline allows the target audience to connect with the professional effortlessly. The headline should entice other professionals to click the professional's profile to learn more about the professional's experience and background. Some professionals miss a key opportunity to connect with prospective professionals by limiting the headline to the professional's title and name of the professional's firm (e.g., Member, XYZ Firm, LLC).

A better headline identifies the professional's area of expertise (e.g., Personal Injury Lawyer). Why? Because a lawyer wants to grab the attention of other professionals examining the lawyer's profile. As important, a lawyer wants to be found by professionals doing a LinkedIn search seeking to connect with a lawyer who specializes in a particular substantive area – like personal injury. Yes, LinkedIn has its own search engine similar to the search engine offered by Google or YouTube, but limited to the database of LinkedIn users. LinkedIn's search engine digests all words in a professional's headline. So, using keywords like "personal injury attorney" helps the search engine pair together the searcher with the professional. In contrast, using a headline of "Partner, XYZ Firm, LLC" does not help the lawyer connect to professionals looking to pair with a personal injury attorney. Finally, a professional's headline appears on other professionals' LinkedIn pages, including keyword search results, newsfeed updates, posted comments, and invitations to connect.

"About" Section

The "About" section appears below the headline and is limited to 2,000 characters, including spaces. But that is sufficient space to pack a powerful punch. A professional should not use the space to present the professional's curriculum vitae. Instead, a professional should use this high-rent space to highlight the professional's skills, experience, and expertise – as well as the professional's passions, motivations, and goals. Weave those facts into a story that describes how the professional can help professionals who are deciding whether to connect with the professional. The professional's target audience should be the focal point of the About section. Describe benefits that professionals in the targeted audience could receive by connecting with the professional.

"Contact Info" Section

A professional should complete the contact information section of the profile to facilitate direct communication between the professional and his/her connections. LinkedIn makes it easy for professionals who are connected to communicate. Clicking the "Contact info" link below the headline opens a box on the screen that can display the professional's linked in address, website address(s), email, twitter handle, and more. This extra information provides multiple ways professionals wishing to connect with a professional can contact the professional. If the contact information section is not completed, then the contacting professional would be limited to messaging through LinkedIn.

Do not worry about privacy. LinkedIn prevents spammers from scraping the professional's profile page for contact emails and phone numbers. Contact and personal information that a professional provides in the contact info section of the profile is only visible to the professional's 1st-degree connections, members to whom the professional has sent a connection invitation (and that invitation is still pending), and members whose InMail(s) the professional has responded to (unless the professional declined their request to share contact info). People the professional emailed before and who have added the professional to their LinkedIn contacts can see the professional's email address. Other information that could be used to contact you, such as your webpage, blog URL or Twitter handle, may be visible to all members.

"Experience" Section

The experience section of a professional's profile is where the professional really shines. Like a curriculum vitae, a professional can present current and past positions. This section adds credibility to a professional's LinkedIn profile. Keywords should be included in the text of the professional's job titles as well as descriptions. Keywords assist the LinkedIn search engine in pairing the professional with professionals searching to make connections.

Sadly, some professionals waste the experience section by disclosing only limited information, such as law firm name, position/title, dates of service, and location. A better approach is to insert keywords that can be found by the LinkedIn search engine so someone searching for those keywords can quickly connect with the professional. For example, a lawyer might use terms like, "personal injury lawyer," "catastrophic injury attorney," or "nursing home injury lawyer" when describing current and past positions.

"Education" Section

The education section is probably the section that is most comfortable for a professional since it closely reflects a curriculum vitae. List the college and law school attended by the professional. For each, list the degree earned and a short description of activities, awards, and accomplishments that may be useful in keyword searches. Do not go overboard and list minor or less significant activities as this can dilute a professional's major achievements.

"Featured" Section

The "Featured" profile element enables professionals to showcase key achievements. This section appears below the "About" section and above the "Experience" section. A professional can feature authored posts, published articles, media like videos, images, documents, and links.

A professional should consider uploading a professionally produced video identifying the benefits of connecting with the professional. Most people considering connecting with the professional will view the video before reading lengthy text.

"Activity" Section

The focus so far has been on the visibility of a professional's profile page. The "Activity" section increases visibility in two way. First, users that are perusing the professional's page can see the professional's activity. Second, a professional's frequent activity facilitates the professional appearing regularly or highly in searches when users type in the keywords the professional is targeting.

A professional needs to be active on LinkedIn to maximize the networking platform's effectiveness. Activity includes comments, shares, likes, and postings. The activity section shows all recent interactions between the professional and his/her connections.

Inactivity diminishes a professional's presence on LinkedIn. a professional's chance of being featured in the

LinkedIn search is reduced due to LinkedIn's algorithm. Inactivity can lead to the professional's connection contacts forgetting the professional exists – with a concomitant reduction in referrals. Plus, an activity feed may not appear in the professional's profile.

Posting

Professionals should post frequently to LinkedIn to keep the professional's connection community engaged. Begin slowly and add substance. Relevant and engaging content is the secret. Professionals should be good at this since law produces mountains of substantive material: court opinions, law reviews, newspaper articles, etc.

A professional can create an image post, video post, or document-based post. Video posts are especially effective as attention grabbers. A professional's article will be published on LinkedIn Pulse, appear in the professional's activity feed, and may show in LinkedIn search when people search for associated keywords. A win-win. Plus, a professional should consider posting a piece of advice (with an appropriate disclaimer), an announcement, firm news, an opinion on a current event, or anything of interest to the professional's network. Staying topical to the professional's practice area is best. Avoid divisive issues like politics.

Multimedia

Multimedia does not have its own section. Instead, many profile sections allow a professional to add multimedia like videos, PDFs, PNGs, GIFs, Power Point pages, Microsoft Word documents, and more. Visual items pique reader attention and lengthen the time a visitor stays on the profile page. Professionals should upload visual media that enhances a professional's story, expertise, past positions, etc. Visual media helps a professional establish a personal brand.

Connection Requests

Building a professional's connection portfolio is job #2 after completing the profile page. To start, LinkedIn will ask for permission to send notice to everyone in a professional's contact list in the address book after a professional registers with LinkedIn. A professional can build his/her connections by asking a user to connect with the professional. LinkedIn makes that easy by offering links to "people who you may know" on the "My Network" page. Each suggested connection will identify a person by name, photo, headline, and number of mutual connections. These people will be connected to the professional's 1st tier of connections or 2nd tier of connections. At the bottom of each suggested connection will be a "Connect" button.

Similarly, LinkedIn offers suggested links in the section labeled "People you may know with similar roles." There too, each suggested connection will identify a person by name, photo, headline, and number of mutual connections. At the bottom of each suggested connection will be a "Connect" button.

To create a connection, the professional must click the "Connect" button. Clicking does not mean that the professional is automatically connected. Instead, clicking sends a message to the prospective connection and essentially asks permission to connect. The user can accept the request, reject the request, or ignore the request. The professional and user only become connected if the user accepts the connection request.

Another way, and perhaps better way, of connecting with someone is to visit the target's LinkedIn profile page and do two things and this order. First, click on the "Message" button appearing just below the banner picture to open a "new message" email box. Add a subject line and write a message identifying the professional. The professional should also indicate why the professional wants to connect and the benefit to the targeted user of connecting with the professional. This email is then sent to the target via the LinkedIn messaging system. Second, the professional should click the blue button labeled "Connect." By clicking, the professional will be sending a connection request to the targeted user. The professional is allowed to add a note to personalize the connection request. A professional should definitely add a personalized note referencing the earlier message and repeating it. Many of the best connections will not agree to connect with someone without receiving the personalized note.

With whom should a professional connect? Connecting with peers is important for credibility, receiving referrals, and staying up to date with industry news. However, connecting directly with potential users who need the professional's service is better.

Paid Advertising

a. Targeting

Advertising on LinkedIn can help a professional achieve his/her goals. LinkedIn allows a professional to target the ideal contacts by various demographic criteria, including job title, company, function, industry, seniority, and more. The targeted contacts will not be other LinkedIn users. Instead, a professional is targeting a quality audience in a professional context. These targets are prospective referral partners.

LinkedIn is an effective marketing tool because the targeting data is reliable since it comes directly from the user. Real professional data for real results. LinkedIn data is differentiated because users have professional incentives to keep their profiles accurate and up-to-date.

Another ideal feature of LinkedIn is the ability to "contact target" to build a customized audience. A professional can market to prospects by securely uploading an email list of contacts or connecting to the professional's contact management platform. Then the professional can deliver relevant content to the customized audience.

Even better, LinkedIn allows retargeting, which allows a professional to segment the audience and deliver unique content based on previous actions the targets have taken with the professional's advertisement. Remarketing accelerates the contact's journey from awareness to conversion as a referral partner.

b. Starting an Advertising Campaign

LinkedIn helps professionals create an advertising campaign that connects the professional's brand to the world's largest audience of active, influential professionals. First, the professional has to create a "Campaign Manager" account at https://www.linkedin .com/campaignmanager/new-advertiser. Campaign Manager allows a professional to set a budget, select goals (clicks v. impressions), and have complete control over the professional's campaign timeline. Campaign Manager offers dynamic visual reporting that recalculates and displays the data that matches the professional's search and filter settings. Campaign Manager also provides a detailed breakout of the actions taken by the ad audience, including Clicks, Likes, Shares, Comments, and Follows. Campaign Manager allows a detailed view of the demographic categories of LinkedIn users who click on the professional's ads.

Second, a professional needs to choose the ad objective that matter most: (a) brand awareness; (b) brand consideration thru website visits, engagements, or video views; and (c) conversion via lead generation, website conversions, or referral partner connections. Brand awareness advertising gets more users to know the professional's brand through impression-based campaigns. Brand consideration advertising gets more users to visit the professional's website. It also drives clicks, social actions, and company page follows. Video view advertising allows the professional to tell his/her story through video. Conversion advertising gets leads using forms pre-filled with LinkedIn member information. Website conversion strategies drive valuable action on the professional's website such as collecting leads or downloading eBooks.

Third, LinkedIn helps a professional reach the right target audience by using LinkedIn's targeting tools for campaign success. Targeting is a foundational element of running a successful advertising campaign. Precise targeting leads to higher engagement, and higher conversion rates. A professional can choose over 20 different audience attribute categories, including the target groups':

- Job title
- Skills
- Job seniority
- School
- Interests
- Groups

c. Choosing the LinkedIn Ad Format

LinkedIn offers templates to create four different advertisement formats: (a) sponsored content; (b) message ads, (c) Dynamic ads, and (d) text ads. Each format is discussed below.

Sponsored content appears directly in the LinkedIn feed of professionals the professional wants to each, and comes in three different formats: single image ads, video ads, and carousel ads. Sponsored content allows a professional to target the most valuable audience population using accurate, profile-based first-party data. Sponsored content also reaches a highly engaged audience with native ads in a professional feed across desktop and mobile devices. Sponsored content drives leads, builds brand awareness, and nurtures key relationships.

Message Ads let a professional reach prospects on LinkedIn Messaging (think email), where they increasingly spend most of their time and where professional conversations happen. A professional can send direct messages to prospects on their Messaging feed to spark immediate action. LinkedIn Messaging drives stronger engagement and response than traditional email marketing. A professional can measure the value in Message Ads by seeing which roles and attributes are taking action on the professional's Message Ads.

Dynamic Ads allows a professional to personalize an advertisement for each targeted member. Dynamic Ads capture attention by featuring each professional's own LinkedIn profile data like photo, company name, job title. The first Dynamic Ad format is the "Follower" ad that promotes a professional's LinkedIn Page or Showcase Page and drives users to follow the professional's LinkedIn page with a single click of the ad from the desktop experience. The second Dynamic Ad format is the "Spotlight," which drives website traffic or sparks an action like event registration. The third Dynamic Ad format is the "Jobs" ad that increases relevant applicants by personalizing ads to top talent on desktop and mobile experiences.

Text Ads are simple but compelling pay-per-click (PPC) or cost-per-impression (CPM) ads.

d. Controlling Costs

A professional sets his/her own budget and can control costs. No contract or long-term commitments is required. The amount a professional pays to advertise on LinkedIn is based on the type of activity selected and the ad "auction." A professional launches an advertising campaign by placing a bid. LinkedIn ads are sold via an ad auction, where the professional's bid competes with other advertisers who want to reach the same target audience. The cost required to win the auction depends on the bid and the desirability of the target audience.

The campaign objective a professional selects determines which ad formats, bidding strategies, and optimization goals are available for the campaign. LinkedIn provides an excellent chart outlining which bid strategies and optimization goas are available for each objective, and how the professional's campaign will be charged based on those selections. The chart can be found at https://business.linkedin.com/content/dam/me/business/en-us/marketing-solutions/cx/2021/images/pdfs/2033_LKIN_PMM_Objective_Based_Pricing_Chart_FY21Q3_V3.pdf.

SECRET 15: YOUTUBE MARKETING

Creating a YouTube channel can dramatically expand a professional's marketing reach. YouTube videos enhance a professional's visibility among a highly targeted audience using limited resources. YouTube can also be used as a highly targeted, low-cost advertising platform that reaches prospects precisely when those prospects are searching for information about services the professional provides. Videos can attract prospects, share testimonials, showcase services, distinguish competitors, and offer tutorials. Google owns YouTube so a professional's chance of being found via a Google search increases with YouTube content.

A professional must define his/her YouTube goals and create videos that specifically help the professional achieve those goals. The primary goal should be to obtain more prospect referrals. No professional will close a deal because of YouTube alone. Prospects should be found through YouTube and closed in the office after the initial consultation. A professional should strive to create engaging, shareable content to grow a referral base.

Statistics

More than ever, prospects are turning to the internet to learn more about professional topics prior to contacting a professional. YouTube is the favored website for some prospects because many prospects find it easier to watch a video about a topic than it is read a blog about the topic or peruse a professional's website. A professional can increase referrals by making it easy for clients to refer family, friends, and contacts to the professional with shareable links in emails and social media to the professional's YouTube videos.

Here are some eye-opening statistics from www.blog. hootsuite.com/youtube-stats-marketers:

- YouTube has more than 2 billion logged-in monthly users.
- 74% of U.S. adults use YouTube.
- 73% of Americans aged 36-45 use YouTube.
- 70% of Americans aged 46-55 use YouTube.
- 56% of YouTube users are male.
- 44% of YouTube users are female.
- YouTube is the world's second-most visited website.
- YouTube is the world's second-most used social platform.
- People watch more than a billion hours of video on YouTube every day.
- 41% of YouTube "watch-time" happens on mobile devices.

Educational & Informational Videos

What type of video might a prospective client be searching to learn more about? The answer is educational and informational videos of course. Nobody looks to professional videos for fun and entertainment. Prospects searching for information are prime prospects.

Another plus to educational and informational videos is that they do not appear to "salesy." Prospects are not looking to be "sold" anything at this point of their research. Overt advertising pitches are too much of a hard sell and can be counterproductive. These types of videos are not scripted like a sales pitch. Instead, the videos provide information without conditions.

Surprisingly, not many professionals employ YouTube marketing, so the marketplace is not saturated. And many of those who do use YouTube marketing are using it to offer a "Free Consultation."

A better YouTube strategy is to create an interesting video that piques a prospect's interest and encourages the prospect to click on a link appearing in the video for a free "special report" that provides more information. The link takes the viewer to the professional's web-based landing page to complete a webform that would provide the special report upon populating the form with the prospect's contact information. The special report is automatically sent to the prospect without consuming any professional time. In return, the populated contact information is sent to the professional via text and email. The professional then contacts the prospect to provide further information and subtly encourage a consultation to discuss the specifics of the prospect's financial situation.

YouTube Strategies

The "special report" strategy suggested above is just one strategy. There are many others. Professionals are limited only by their imagination, creativity, ingenuity, and budget. YouTube can be used to implement a myriad of strategies. Some are listed below:

- Generate new prospects.
- Share client endorsements and testimonials.
- Enhance a professional's credibility.
- Boost a firm's brand awareness.
- Advertise an existing service.
- Introduce details about a new professional service.
- Share details about a professional's curriculum vitae.
- Educate prospects on the benefits of professional action.

- Differentiate a professional's services from competitors.
- Share the firm's mission.
- Tell the professional's story, his/her history, philosophy, and goals.
- Share video footage of presentations given.
- Broadcast and stream live events.

Common Traits of Successful Videos

No universal formula works for all professionals. Videos come in all shapes and sizes depending upon the strategy and goals of the professional. But certain traits are common in successful campaigns.

First, professionals should strive to keep the video short and focused. A video should use the first few seconds to convey what the video is about and why the viewer should watch it. Six minutes should be the maximum length.

The professional's "call to action" should be displayed near the beginning of the video and then repeated near the middle and again at the end. Repeated display allows the viewer to click the hyperlinking button when the viewer feels the impulse. Do not make the viewer wait until the end of the video. Allow the viewer to strike (take action) when the iron is hot.

The professional must include the professional's name and contact information in the video's description and embed the information in the video footage itself. Name and contact information can be identified via voice-over, featured in the video, or titles or captions. Using the copyright symbol is recommended to scare away villains who want to pirate the professional's video and brand it as their own.

A successful video focuses on a pre-defined goal and targets a specific audience. The professional should strive to create content that is unique and differentiates the professional from competitors. YouTube viewers are quick to judge whether a video is worth spending the time watching. A professional should offer content that is perceived as useful, informative, educational, entertaining, and relevant to what the viewer is searching for in the YouTube search engine.

Developmental Techniques

Developmental techniques must be considered before a professional starts creating the first video. These techniques improved the "visibility" of the professional's videos in the YouTube search engine as well as the Google search engine. These techniques also make the videos more pleasing to view and more potent for developing prospects.

A professional must tap his/her creativity to present the message and call to action in a way that achieves his/her objective. Here are some video elements to consider:

- Live-action video of people, places, and things.
- Music and sound effects.
- Graphic titles using text.
- Charts and graphics.
- Visual special effects.
- Animation.
- Text overlaying live-action.
- Screen shots with voice-overlays.
- Interactive "cards" that hyperlink to professional's website.

Video creation must be developed around a professional's core message that must be consistently conveyed through the video to the viewers. A professional's core message must be carefully crafted for the audience – short, memorable, and easily understandable. Before beginning, a professional must determine what action the professional wants the viewer to take while watching the video or afterwards. The professional directs the viewer to take the action with a "call to action" button (e.g., "Schedule Your Appointment Now by Calling 555-555-5555.") that hyperlinks to the professional's website.

a. Keyword Research

A professional must perform keyword research to uncover the video content for which prospects are searching. Keywords are ideas and topics that define what the video content is about. In terms of SEO, they are the words and phrases that prospects enter into search engines, also called "search queries." A professional's videos should be designed around those keywords.

A great resource for conducting keyword research is TubeBuddy Tags (www.TubeBuddy.com). TubeBuddy is a free Chrome browser extension/browser plugin that adds a layer of tools directly on top of YouTube's website. The extension allows a professional to check the keywords competitors are using for their videos. A professional new to YouTube can piggy-back on the expensive research done by more experienced competitors.

b. Script Writing

Professionals should invest time in creating a well-crafted script that conveys empathy while providing information. What a professional says is critical. The prospect will be listening, unlike Facebook videos that are typically watched without sound. Scripts need clean intros and good talking points.

A good script should include a summary of what will be covered and then introduce the subject of the video very early to keep prospects viewing. A professional should be as conversational as possible and avoid legalese. Save the legal jargon for the bar association meetings. Keep sentences short and to the point. Be friendly and approachable so that a prospect can envision himself/herself consulting with the attorney.

c. Educational Content

More and more prospects are turning to the internet for information before they are ready to engage a professional. Prospects use YouTube to learn. Research has shown prospects are 4X more likely to watch educational or informational videos than they are to read text. That is where YouTube's videos may beat Google's text. Research also reveals that how-to videos earn the most attention of any content category on YouTube, even more than music clips and gaming.

Professionals should tailor their videos to match the information prospects are looking for when conducting searches. These videos must answer the questions the prospects are asking. Providing information and answering questions builds authority and trust. Viewers are more likely to contact the attorney after viewing videos because of that authority and trust.

d. Testimonials

YouTube should be used to host client testimonials that are embedded on a professional's website. Testimonial videos build trust and calm a prospect's anxiety about contacting the professional. Contacting a professional can be an anxiety riddled step into the unknown world of law, professionals, and the court system. A prospect is more likely to engage the professional after viewing testimonial videos because the professional becomes trusted to guide the prospect through the unknown world of law.

Positive client testimonials help to establish a professional's credibility and reliability. Testimonials are perhaps the most important content on a professional's website and should be located on the homepage. Testimonials build trust and prove to prospects that the professional's claims on the website are supported by real client experiences that mirror the prospects' situations.

e. Call-to-Action

Every video should have a "call to action." A call to action is a marketing term for any design that prompts an immediate response or encourages an immediate action. A call to action in the YouTube context is a prompt on a video that instructs the viewer to take some specified action. A call to action is typically written as a command or action phrase, such as "Call Now" and generally takes the form of a button hyperlinking the viewer to the professional's website.

A professional cannot assume that a prospect knows what to do after watching the video. Without a call to action, a viewer might stay on YouTube and watch a competitor's video without contacting the professional. Simply identifying the professional's firm at the conclusion of the video is insufficient. Direct the prospect to the next step.

Calls to action should appear multiple times in a longer video and at least twice in a shorter 1 to 5-minute video. Add the call-to-action command/link in multiple locations for longer videos because viewers may not watch the entire video when longer than a few minutes. Add the call-to-action command/link in the middle of the video and again at the end for shorter videos.

The call to action must be easy to understand, specific, and succinct. Examples of good calls to action include:

- Call Now at 312-555-5555.
- Need help? Call us at 312-555-5555.
- Schedule an appointment now at 312-555-5555.
- Click here for more information.
- Visit our website for more information.

f. Website "About Us" Video

The professional should have a video on the website's "About Us" page to build a brand, and not be "just another professional." The video's central thrust should be the key value proposition that distinguishes the attorney from competitors and causes the prospect to contact the attorney. All though out, the video should convey credibility and authority while sharing the story of who the professional is and why the professional wants to help prospects. For example, a lawyer could share his passion for personal injury because he helped his own brother obtain personal injury compensation when in need and realized the positive impact on his brother's life.

g. Search Engine Optimization (SEO)

SEO occurs immediately after a video is uploaded to YouTube. A professional must summarize the video before it is made public. That summary is the key to impactful SEO and includes the title, description, tags, and keywords.

A video's title should include the professional's main target keyword once. The title should also be intriguing enough to entice viewers to click the link to watch the video. The description should be 300 or more words and include the main keyword. A longer description is better because it provides YouTube with a solid understanding of the video content and helps potential viewers decide whether to watch it.

Video "tags" should be used. Tags are descriptive keywords used to help viewers find content that matches their viewing needs. Make sure the video tags are accurate to avoid being penalized in the rankings. Do not include a tag on the most popular issue of current world events when the video is about estate planning only.

h. Transcripts

Professionals should include a complete transcript of each video when uploading a video to YouTube. Search engine results will increase because search engines crawl website text to index sites. Search engines are able to crawl a video more effectively when transcriptions are provided. Transcripts allow the professional to use the all-important keywords in a natural way as a supplement to video titles, descriptions, and tags.

More serious viewers may be interested in reading the video transcript to better understand the video content. Some viewers are reading/writing learners while others are visual/auditory learners. Give prospects both and let them decide.

i. Video Duration

Law is serious business. Prospects hunt for information on law only when they are in serious financial condition. Prospects are not looking for 60 second videos at that time.

Rather, prospects are looking for depth in educational and information videos. Spend the time and extend the video duration to build credibility and trust.

Longer viewing by prospects also helps search rankings. In depth videos increase total watch time per video and total time viewers are on the professional's website. Both of these are ranking factors.

j. Animation

Animation catches a viewer's eye and can be intriguing when done correctly. Listening to a professional talk may be the opposite of catchy animation. Animation usually includes a voice-over by the professional explaining complex issues. Animation can allow a prospect to visualize the various steps of the process without having to listen to the professional who is standing in front of a camera.

k. Approach

Some professionals are more outgoing than other professionals. At least one lawyer quit law to become a stand-up comedian. The gift of gab can be useful. This type of lawyer should consider promoting himself/herself as an online personality that entertains the audience. An outgoing professional can be the featured speaker and build rapport with the viewers while simultaneously personalizing the professional's brand. It can effective if genuine or a disaster if forced.

For most professionals, sincerity is the best approach. Be genuine. These professionals feature themselves to provide background information about their firm, tell their story, build their brand, and inform prospects about their professional services. They can build virtual relationships that are not possible with text ladened websites.

Publishing Platforms

Synergy is the name of the game. Everything a professional does online should be synergistic. All platforms should be fully integrated and cross pollinated focusing relentlessly on the professional's core message. A professional should publish videos on YouTube, of course, and all other places on the web and social media where the targeted audience may be gathering information. A professional's main website has already been discussed but do not forget landing pages. LinkedIn can be great for generating referrals, and Avvo can be effective too.

Videos are effective in Facebook ads and on a professional's business page and in newsfeeds. In fact, Facebook engagement is substantially higher on Facebook posts that include video content. Ads are more effective when incorporated into video. Research shows that Facebookers are 27X more likely to click a post that contains video than on a static banner ad.

One problem with Facebook is muting. Many people access their Facebook account via a cell phone with the noise muted. Some are at the office, some commuting, and some at home. The default appears to be muted viewing. That is a problem if the video format is a single person talking directly at the camera. A viewer would not hear the content and may click away from the video. Adjust the video accordingly, including using text blocks and graphics. More tech sophisticated professionals can try animation.

Facebook advertising that incorporates video content can be great for driving traffic to the professional's homepage for more information or to the professional's landing page designed to obtain the prospect's contact information.

Creating a Channel

A professional must create a YouTube "channel" before a video can be uploaded. Think of the "channel" like an electronic filing cabinet controlled by the professional. A professional should properly brand the channel with the professional's logo and other related graphics or channel art. Then, the professional should enter a channel description informing viewers what to expect by following the professional on the YouTube channel. Finally, videos are uploaded to the professional's channel and viewers use the YouTube search engine to locate the video.

Professionals who sign-up for a Google Gmail account are automatically granted access to a unique YouTube account associated with that Gmail account. But beware of compromising the privacy of the professional's personal Gmail account if the professional will have staff who needs access to the channel to upload videos. A better idea is to create a different Gmail account used solely for YouTube matters to maintain the professional's privacy with the personal Gmail account.

Analytics

Utilize the online tool set called YouTube Analytics. These tools help professional's track information about who is watching the professional's videos by many metrics including the following:

- Traffic source.
- Viewer age.
- Viewer gender.
- Views per date.
- Device type.

Promotion

Professionals have to learn to generate organic traffic by promoting their YouTube videos using free advertising to build a stronger channel. Videos should be embedded in the professional's website as well as featured on a Facebook page, blog, and the professional's online social networking services. Search engine optimization is a tall hill to climb but it will pay dividends.

Below are a dozen proven strategies for promoting a professional's videos:

1. Use all the tools offered by YouTube to increase visibility with the YouTube search engine. A professional should start with keyword research to determine the most common search terms used for the segment of the population the professional is targeting. Then the professional should utilize the keywords when creating a title for a video. Similarly, the professional incorporates keywords into the video description and tags. Search engine optimization (SEO) is important to expand the reach of a professional's videos.

2. Create an attention-getting thumbnail image to showcase the video. YouTube is a visual medium in which viewers decide whether to watch a video after only getting a glimpse of the video. Making a good first impression has never been as important as the thumbnail image. A viewer may not watch a video that has a poor thumbnail image.

Every video has a thumbnail image by definition. The professional is allowed to upload an image and should do so. Hire a professional graphic designer to create an image. YouTube will create its own thumbnail image of the video if the professional fails to upload an image. The thumbnail image created by YouTube is a snapshot of a random film cell taken from the professional's video. But which cell YouTube selects is part of its algorithm. It could be a great shot of the professional smiling or a shot with the professional's eyes closed – or worse. A professional should not leave the quality of the thumbnail image to chance by allowing YouTube to select an image. Instead, a professional should make the effort to upload a quality thumbnail image that will intrigue a viewer into watching the video.

3. Use a call-to-action to direct viewers to take whatever action the professional pre-selected. Some professionals want to build a YouTube channel so they direct viewers to "like" their videos, share their videos with friends, or comment on the videos. Other professionals encourage viewers to subscribe to their channel.

One of the best calls to action encourages viewers to click a hypertext link that takes viewers to the professional's landing page on the firm website, which is specifically tailored to viewers who click on the hypertext link. The landing page can have further text providing information plus a webform to gather contact information like name, email address, cell phone number, etc.

4. Direct promotion to family, friends, and contacts is key. A professional should start any promotion efforts with the people who know the professional best. Then ask each of these people to contact their respective family, friends, and contacts and provide a link to the video(s) or link to the professional's YouTube channel page.

5. Social media should be an integral part of a professional's promotion strategy. Videos are great for posting on Facebook, Twitter, Instagram, and other services.

6. YouTube videos should be embedded into a professional's website. The homepage is the perfect location for a video introducing the professional, showing empathy, describing the firm's mission, and otherwise humanizing the professional. A video featuring client testimonials is a must to develop trust between prospects and the professional. The "about us" page should also have a video that builds creditability. Other videos should be considered – including FAQ videos.

7. Incorporate YouTube videos into a professional's blog. Many prospects view a professional's blog to learn about professional issues prior to contacting the professional for a consultation. Professionals may like reading lengthy passages, but prospects typically do not. Rather, allow prospects to view videos instead of reading text.

8. Seek out other bloggers to cross-promote a professional's videos. Ask other bloggers to discuss the professional's videos or feature the videos on the blogger's blog. The professional should reciprocate and return the favor to those bloggers to help expand the bloggers' reach.

8. Professionals should amend their email signature block to add a link to the professional's YouTube channel. That way every email sent is a promotional plug.

9. Employ press releases to contact editors and reporters to generate free media coverage for a professional's videos. Consider embracing public relations techniques to contact TV and radio producers for the same reason.

10. Pay for advertising on YouTube and other search engines to quickly generate views.

11. Utilize "cards" and "end screens" within each video to promote a professional and the professional's website.

These devices hyperlink to the professional's website, including any landing pages.

12. Create "playlists" that comprise a collection of related videos produced by the professional. Playlists can suggest an appropriate order for watching the videos. It also encourages a viewer to watch videos back-to-back, which increases the likelihood that the viewer will follow the professional's call to action prompts.

Paid Advertising / Keyword Advertising

Professionals can use YouTube in a myriad of methods. A professional can use paid advertising on YouTube to drive traffic to the professional's website. Professionals should consider a YouTube paid advertising campaign.

Paid advertising includes both text-based ads and display ads. A more creative professional can create a video message that resembles a 15 to 60-second TV commercial that stands on its own or serves as a prologue to another video. Professionals can even use paid placements with a YouTuber with a mass following.

Paid advertising works quickly and is relatively inexpensive when the advertising is highly targeted. Paid advertising is sometimes called keyword advertising because it allows a professional's ad to be seen at the exact moment a prospect is searching for content based on a keyword or search phrase that matches a keyword associated with the professional's video content or channel. Paid advertising usually works on a pay-per-click (PPC) or pay-per-view (PPV) basis. With PPC, a professional incurs a cost only when a viewer clicks on the ad.

1. Video Discovery Ads

Video discovery ads (VDAs) are stand-alone ads that appear on the YouTube homepage. VDAs also appear within search results much like Adwords advertisements appear on a Google search results page. VDAs also appear as related videos on YouTube video watch pages. These ads show a thumbnail image with text. The image and text are hyperlinks to the professional's promoted video. A viewer clicks on the ad to be redirected to the video.

2. In-Stream Ads

Unlike video discovery ads that are stand-alone ads, in-stream ads (ISAs) play in conjunction with a YouTube video selected by a viewer after conducting a YouTube search. ISAs can be customized with overlay text and calls to action.

ISA ads can play either before the search targeted video or during the search targeted video. ISAs that play before the viewer watches the search targeted video are called pre-roll in-stream ads. These are skippable video ads that allow viewers to skip the ad after watching the first five seconds. ISAs that play during the search targeted video are called mid-roll videos and typically appear midway through YouTube videos that are 10 minutes in length or longer.

3. Non-Skippable Ads

Some ads are skippable after the view watches the first 5 seconds of a video. However, other ads are non-skippable video ads. These non-skippable ads must be watched before a video can be viewed. These ads are typically 15 or 20 seconds in length.

As a final thought about YouTube, strive to use video marketing as only one part of a larger marketing campaign.

Consider the synergistic effect of using YouTube in conjunction with other social marketing platforms. Incorporate videos everywhere professionals market. Add links to emails, add links to webpages, add links to blogs. Cross-promote and enjoy the rewards.

SECRET 16: GOOGLE ADS MARKETING

Google dominates the search engine market with a market share exceeding 90%. Google offers professionals an opportunity to appear in its Google search results – for a fee – through its Google Ads advertising system. In 2018, Google changed the name of its advertising system form "Google AdWords" to "Google Ads." Professionals bid to display brief advertisements, service offerings, or videos to web users. It can place ads both in the results of search engines like Google Search and on non-search websites, mobile apps, and videos.

Google Ads provides professionals with the power to reach their target audience with relevant advertising messages. Google Ads allows professionals to measure the results of an advertising campaign and tweak underperforming advertisements for enhanced performance. Google Ads allows professionals to maintain control of the advertising budget.

The beauty of Google Ads is the immediacy of the platform. A professional can cause a display ad to appear on a prospect's search result who is actively looking for professional information. This allows the professional's display ad to be shown to prospects when they are most likely to be receptive to the professional's marketing message.

Google Ads offers range of targeting options that allows professionals to pinpoint their prospects. One example is targeting by geographic location of the searchers. A professional who provides professional services locally is able to focus the advertising budget on searchers who live in the professional's service area.

Professionals can advertise on a small budget with Google Ads, which is not possible with traditional media like newspapers, TV, or magazines. Google Ads does not require a minimum advertising commitment. A professional can start advertising on a small budget and then increase the advertising budget as the professional engages more and more clients. Better yet, a professional is only charged when prospects engage with the professional's advertisements and click on the ad that links to the professional's landing page. A professional is not billed when a searcher reads a professional's ad (an impression) but does not click on the advertisement. The professional can also adjust how much the professional wants to spend on clicks by limiting the visibility of ads to particular days and/or time of day.

Another trait that pushes Google Ads to the top of a professional's advertising campaign is the professional's ability to make adjustments to a campaign ad. Traditional media have sunk costs relating to the production and display of advertising. No changes are allowed without a large expenditure. Not true with paid search. A professional can make changes at any time to the ad copy so that the ads are up-to-date. Many professionals implement A/B testing to determine which ad has a better response rate.

A professional has the ability to choose when his/her ads are shown. This flexibility allows the professional to show ads on particular days or during particular hours.

Last, Google Ads allows a professional to measure the results of an advertising campaign to better understand which ad copy is working and which copy is not working. Statistics allow the professional to make adjustments to improve the advertising campaign performance so that the professional can spend the advertising budget advertising to the best audience at the best time.

AdWords Account Structure

A professional has to create an "account" with Google to implement a Google Ads marketing strategy. The account settings establish billing information and limit control of the account to designated people, among other things.

A professional's account contains one or more "campaigns." Each campaign serves as a folder in which various "ad groups" are stored. Campaign folders provide structure for a professional's overall Google Ads marketing strategy. A professional could have 10 or more different advertisements running simultaneously with Google Ads and the lack of organization could prove disastrous. Google created the "campaign" folders to help professionals stay organized.

A professional can create one or more "ad groups" within a campaign. Each ad group serves as a sub-folder withing the campaign folder. Each ad group contains (a) keywords that the professional has selected, and (b) the ads that the professional is displaying to users who Google those keywords. Such organizational emphasis may seem like overkill for professionals new to Google Ads who are planning a single ad – and it is if the professional is only going to use one ad. But organization is key when a professional expands the marketing campaign with multiple ads, if not scores of ads. The ad group concept allows a professional to refine the structure of a campaign and enables the professional to be more granular with ad targeting and analyzing.

Keywords

Keyword is defined in the dictionary as a "word or concept of great significance." Google defines keyword differently. Google says a keyword is a word or phrase describing a professional's service that the professional chooses to help determine when and where the professional's ad can appear in Google search results.

The keywords a professional chooses are used to show the professional's ads to people. A professional should select high-quality, relevant keywords for an ad campaign to help the professional reach only the most interested people, who are more likely to become your clients.

When someone searches on Google, the professional's ad could be eligible to appear based on the similarity of the keywords to the person's search terms, as well as the keyword match types. Keywords can also be used to match the professional's ads to sites in the Google Network that are related to your keywords and ads.

Keyword selection is an art more than a science. The keyword industry has mushroomed to include keyword "experts" who claim they have insight into the Google search engine algorithm. Keyword selection is perhaps the most important aspect of a Google Ads campaign. A great keyword list can help improve the performance of a professional's ads and help avoid higher prices. Poor keyword lists can ultimately cause the professional to pay higher prices and receive lower ad positions.

When determining the correct keywords, a professional should ask a simple question: "what search terms would a non-professional type into the Google search engine when searching for a divorce professional?" The question is easy, the answer is not. First, professionals have a separate vocabulary that is not used by typical prospects. Omit words that are not within a prospect's lexicon. Second, a professional should ask clients what terms they entered into the Google search engine. Plus, a professional should ask family and friends what terms they would use. Third, there are websites that help professionals select keywords. For example, see the following websites: www.adwords.google.com/ keywordplanner and www.landing.semrush.com/keyword-research-tool-3/usa.html.

One strategy is to shy away from generic terms like "lawyer" or "divorce lawyer" since these keywords are astronomically expensive and only attorneys with deep marketing pockets can afford a marketing fight in that arena. A better strategy may be focus on long-tail keywords that consist of four or more words a searcher may string together in a Google query. For example, "divorce lawyer offering free consultation" and "file divorce today to protect children" are long-tail keywords. The bidding price for long-tail keywords is much more affordable than generic terms. A lawyer should be as specific as possible to attract prospects that are interested in the lawyer's services and not just browsing for general information. The easiest way to draft keywords is to consider a prospect's intent when conducting a Google search. Draft the keywords the prospect would use if that prospect wanted to hire a professional and not just learn more information about the professional process.

Google Ads "Smart" Campaign

Google Ads "Smart" campaigns must be distinguished from Google Ads "Search" campaigns. "Smart" campaigns differ from "Search" campaigns by the degree of control afforded the professional. With Google Ads Smart Campaign, the professional's options are limited by a single ad format, a single business's category, and keywords chosen by Google. Whereas, with Google Ads Search Campaigns, the professional controls most everything about the campaign. A professional may be served better by choosing Google Ads "Search" campaigns instead of Google Ads "Smart" Campaigns. Nevertheless, a discussion of Google Ads Smart

Campaigns is set forth below and a discussion of Google Ads Search Campaigns is set forth in the following section.

In Google AdsSmart Campaigns, the professional sets up an account, builds a single ad, selects the professional's business category, sets a budget, and that is it! The professional can see what keywords Google has chosen for the professional, but the professional cannot adjust them (match type or bidding).

A professional starts a new Google Ads Smart Campaign by going to his/her Google Gmail account and clicking on the Google app launcher on the top menu bar to the left of the professional's picture, which looks like a square consisting of three rows of three black dots. A grey circle illuminates behind the dots when the professional hovers over the dots. Next, scroll down to find the app titled "Google Ads" and click on it. The professional is taken to the "Grow your business with Google Ads" page. https://ads.google.com/home/?subid=ww-ww-et-g-aw-a-vasquette_ads_cons_1!o2&authuser=1#!/ Click the "start now" button to begin the Google Ads step-by-step campaign creation tool.

Google asks the professional to identify the business name on the first screen. The second screen asks for the professional's website address where the professional wants a searcher to land. This could be the professional's home page or a special "landing page" designed for a particular campaign. The app searches the web for the professional's selected webpage and displays the site on the computer screen.

Google Ads helps a professional write an ad by offering suggestions for Headline 1, Headline 2, and Headline 3. If the offered suggestions are unappealing, then the professional can change them to whatever the professional desires as long as each of the headlines is 30 or fewer characters. The same is true of the Description 1 line and the Description 2 line – however their limitation is 90 characters each. A professional is also offered an optional "show a call button in your ad" feature. Google Ads provides visual help by displaying a sample ad copy layout so that a professional can visualize how the ad would appear to prospects searching for professional help.

The next screen focuses on adding keyword themes to match the professional's ad to searches. A single keyword theme represents multiple similar words and phrases. For instance, the keyword theme "divorce lawyer" may make a lawyer's ad eligible to show when people search for "divorce lawyer near me," or "local divorce lawyer," and "aggressive divorce lawyer."

The professional's next screen focuses on the location in which the ad will appear. Two radio buttons are provided: advertise near an address, and advertise in specific zip codes, cities, or regions. An input box is provided when the professional wants to narrow the advertising to a specific zip code, city, or region.

The professional is allowed to set a monthly budget. Google Ads also offers three suggested budget alternatives. Once entered, Google Ads estimates the number of clicks each month.

Google Ads allows the professional to review the campaign to guarantee all the imputed information is correct. Changes can be made at this time. If accurate, the professional is taken to the "Confirm payment info" page where the professional's credit card information is confirmed from billing information previously inserted when the professional created the Google account.

The final step is to click the blue "Submit" button to initiate the Google Ads Smart Campaign.

Google Ads "Search" Campaign

Google Ads Search Campaigns differ from Google Ads Smart Campaigns by the degree of control afforded the professional. With Google Ads Search Campaigns, the professional controls most everything about the campaign. Whereas, with Google Ads Smart Campaign, the professional's options are limited by a single ad format, a single business's category, and keywords chosen by Google.

Google Ads Search Campaigns drive prospects to the professional's website home page or specially designed landing page. Search ads allow the attorney to highlight key information about the professional or firm. Google tracks the progress of a professional's search campaign with dashboard analytics. A professional can easily create multiple versions of the same text ad and apply A/B testing to optimize results.

A professional starts a new Google Ads Search Campaign by going to his/her Google Gmail account and clicking on the Google app launcher on the top menu bar to the left of the professional's picture, which looks like a square consisting of three rows of three black dots. A grey circle illuminates behind the dots when the professional hovers over the dots. Next, scroll down to find the app titled "Google Ads" and click on it. The professional is taken to the "Grow your business with Google Ads" page. https://ads.google.com/home/?subid=ww-ww-et-g-aw-a-vasquette_ads_cons_1!o2&authuser=1#!/

Do not click the "start now" button. Instead, navigate to the main menu and click on the menu item labeled "Advanced campaigns" to link to a page titled "Discover the right solutions for your marketing objective." Here the professional selects a marketing objective from a pre-defined list: sales, leads, website traffic, product and brand consideration, brand awareness and reach, and app promotion.

Most professionals would probably select "website traffic" as their objective by clicking on the icon. Continue to navigate down the same page and click the box "Search Campaigns" to reach people interested in professional services. A blue "Learn more" link appears. A professional should click the link to educate himself/herself on creating a search ad, choosing the best audience, and setting a budget.

By scrolling further down the same page, a professional finds six helpful tools that can help make a search campaign more effective. These tools are Keyword Planner, Google Ads Editor, Manager Accounts, Performance Planner, Google Ads Mobile App, and Reach Planner. Each tool is presented inside its own box on the webpage. A click of a box reveals a "Learn more" link for a fuller explanation of that tool. Best practices suggest clicking on all tools to discover possibilities.

The Keyword Planner helps a professional find the keywords that are most relevant for professionals. Google's keyword research tool gives a professional insight into how often certain words are searched and how those searches have changed over time. The keyword planner gives suggested estimates for each keyword to help determine an appropriate budget.

Google Ads Editor helps a professional create an ad and then edit the ad from the comfort of the professional's desktop. The editor tool allows a professional to download a campaign and work on it even when offline. The editor tool also displays a draft ad copy. This tool tracks important campaign metrics, including click-through rate, cost, position, and conversion information.

The Performance Planner offers auction data, seasonality trends, and other signals to show how changes to a professional's campaign might affect performance. Performance Planner allows a professional to determine the right budget for a campaign. It forecasts campaign performance and allows a professional to see the impact of adjusting a campaign setting or the budget. The planner offers metrics on clicks, conversions, and cost-per-action.

A professional can start a Google Ads Search Campaign by clicking the blue "Start Now" button at the bottom of the same page as all the information above – directly below Google's call to action phrase: "Achieve your marketing objectives today." The professional is taken to a page titled "What's your main advertising goal?" Three boxes containing different objectives appear below the title with a blue "Next" button below the boxes. Do NOT click the button because it will take the professional to the Google Ads Smart Campaign tools and not the Google Ads Search Campaign tools.

A professional wishing to start a search campaign needs to click the link below the Next button: "Are you a professional marketer? Switch to Expert Mode." That link begins the search campaign by directing a professional to select the goal that would make the search campaign successful. The professional is given 8 objectives, each contained within a separate box. Most professionals would probably click the "Website traffic" box causing a new set of decision boxes to appear on the same page. The professional is directed to select a campaign type from a list of two alternative ad types: search or display. A professional would probably click the "Search" box. That selection causes another box to appear at the bottom of the screen directing the professional to "Select the ways you'd like to reach your goal." This step helps customize the campaign setup to focus on settings and features that can help the professional get the customer actions that matter most. The professional should insert a website home page URL or landing page URL in this box.

The final box on the page allows a professional to start tracking website traffic as website conversions. A conversion action is something valuable to the professional that people do after interacting with the professional's ads. To track website traffic as conversion actions across the professional's account, the professional must create a conversion action and then install the tracking code. Thankfully, Google offers a link to create a conversion action. The page concludes by clicking the "Continue" button at the bottom of the page.

a. Step 1 Select Campaign Settings.

Now the professional is ready to start focusing on selecting the campaign "Settings." The professional should create a unique campaign name that suggests the focus of the campaign. A professional would probably have more than one campaign and could have dozens of them. A unique name minimizes confusion and enhances organization.

Next, the professional focuses on the networks in which the ads will be displayed: search network and display network. A professional should consider de-selecting the checked box in the Search Network section that is titled "Include Google search partners." Similarly, a professional should consider de-selecting the checked box in the Display Network section titled "Include Google Display Network." By de-selecting the boxes, the professional directs the ads to appear in Google search results instead of diluting the campaign across multiple Google controlled partners.

The professional must toggle the accordion "Show more settings" arrow to reveal several key settings. First, the professional can control the start and end dates of the search campaign. The default setting is to continue running ads in perpetuity. Second, the professional can insert a campaign URL option that serves as a tracking template. A tracking template lets a professional put additional information in the URL to identify the source of an individual ad click. For example, professional can add URL parameters that will tell which campaign and ad group contained the ad that the user clicked on, what type of device the user was on, and which keyword triggered the ad. Most professionals do not need to set up a tracking template because the aggregate performance statistics, like how many clicks did a campaign and ad group deliver, how many clicks did a keyword trigger, or how many clicks occurred from a mobile vs. desktop device, are sufficient.

Third, a professional can enter a dynamic search ad setting that targets relevant searches automatically based on the professional's website, then use headlines automatically customized to users' actual searches. This setting determines what domain, language, and targeting source to use.

Fourth, a professional can control the ad schedule that determines when the ad will run. The default is "All days" and all times. Click the "All days" accordion arrow to control the days and click the "00:00" accordion arrows to control the time of day the campaign will start and end.

The next setting relates to "Targeting and audiences" the professional wants to reach with the search ads. The United States radio button is the default. Best practices suggest clicking on the radio button labeled "Enter another location" to reveal a field to enter a target location like a state, city, town, or zip code. For example, a professional can enter DuPage County, IL and Google will identify the ad reach as 2,050,000 people. The professional can then choose to "exclude" part of that audience. Assume the professional chooses to exclude that subset of DuPage County that is located within the 60521 zip code area. To do that, the professional would exclude "60521" and Google would identify the 60521 subgroup as 292,000 people. By clicking "exclude," the professional would exclude those people living in the 60521 zip code area. Thus, the professional's ad, as modified, would be available to all people living in DuPage County, IL except those living in the subset of DuPage County that comprises the 60521 zip code area – a target group comprising 1,758,000 people (2,050,000 – 292,000 = 1,758,000).

Below that is a "Location options" accordion arrow. Click on it to reveal the "Target" with three alternative radio buttons. The first button is labeled "Presence or interest" for searchers in, regularly in, or who have shown interest in the professional's targeted location. The second button is labeled "Presence" for searchers located in or regularly in the professional's targeted locations. The third button is labeled "Search interest" for searchers who are searching for the professional's targeted locations. A professional should consider clicking the second radio button "Presence" to avoid paying for clicks from searchers who do not live in the professional's geographically targeted area.

The next setting section is budget. This section defines how much a professional wants to spend and how the professional wants to spend it. The first subpart is the budget. The professional must identify the average amount to be spent each day, which in turn sets the maximum monthly amount to be spent. For the month, the professional will not pay more than the daily budget times the average number of days in a month. Some days the professional might spend less than the daily budget, and on other days the professional might spend up to twice as much.

The daily average budget concept needs further explanation. Internet traffic is like an ocean. Some days, there will be small waves. Other days, there will be great big ones. So, if a professional's ads do not show up much because of low traffic, then Google will make up for that by showing them more when traffic is higher. That is why Google allows up to 2 times the clicks in a day than the average daily budget allows for campaigns that are not paying for conversions. This is called "over-delivery." If Google ends up showing an ad too much -- to the point where the professional accrues more costs than the average daily budget allows for over a billing cycle -- then Google will give the professional a credit for those extra costs. Over a month-long billing cycle, the professional will not be charged more than the average daily budget would have allowed for the month.

The bidding section instructs the Google Ads tool to focus on various types of campaigns. A professional should consider selecting the "Clicks" campaign. By doing so, the tool will implement the "maximize clicks" bid strategy to help the professional get the most clicks for the budget.

More savvy Google Ads marketers should consider clicking on the link at the bottom of the "Bidding" box that is labeled "Or, select a bid strategy directly (not recommended)". This link changes the bidding from the recommended "Clicks" bid initiative controlled by Google's algorithm to a bid strategy controlled by the professional. The professional has six automated bid strategies to choose from and each is described in a separate section: Target CPA, Target ROAS, Maximize clicks, Maximize conversions, Maximize conversion value, and Target impression Share. The professional also has a manual bid strategy option called Manual CPC.

Finally, a professional is allowed to direct the ad rotation when multiple ads are used in a campaign. The default radio button is titled "Optimize," which prefers the best performing ads. These are the ads that are expected to get more clicks. The second radio button is the "Do not optimize" that rotates ads indefinitely despite poor performance. Best practices suggest allowing the Google tool to optimize the ads unless the professional has a reason to do otherwise. Finally, the professional advances the campaign creation process by clicking the blue "Save and Continue" button.

b. Step 2 Set Up Ad Groups

A campaign consists of one or more ad groups. An ad group contains one or more ads and a set of related keywords. Some Google Ads pros believe each ad group should contain all the ads and keywords on one type of service – like estate planning. A different ad group can contain all the ads and keywords on a different type of service – like tax.

Best practices suggest using a unique ad group for each of the professional's best keywords so that the professional can control the ad copy triggered by the keyword and the corresponding landing page for that keyword. Another benefit of a single keyword ad group is the professional's control over keyword bidding and the keyword's quality score generated by the Google algorithm. The quality score assesses the relevance of the professional's keywords to the campaign.

A professional must select the most desirable ad group type. Ad group types determine the kind of ads and targeting options a professional has within an ad group. The standard ad group type utilizes text ads written by the professional that serve based on the keywords the professional selects. In contract, the dynamic ad group type utilizes text ads that use the professional's website content to target relevant searches and generate headlines automatically. Google believes that dynamic ads are the easiest way to find clients searching on Google for precisely what the professional offers. Perhaps ideal for advertisers with a well-developed website or a large inventory, Dynamic Search Ads use website content to target ads and can help fill in the gaps of keyword-based campaigns. Dynamic Search Ad headlines and landing pages are also generated using content from the professional's website, which keeps ads relevant and saves the professional time. Best practices suggest utilizing the standard ad group type for a professional with a less complex website.

Next, a professional must create a name for the first ad group. Be as specific as possible to enhance organization. Keyword selection comes immediately below. Keyword targeting can put an ad in front of interested users and increase a professional's return on investment (ROI). Google offers keywords (words and phrases) that are used to match a professional's ads with the terms used by people conducting Google searches. These keywords are generated from Google's scan of the professional's website. A professional can also identify various services provided to generate additional keywords. Now comes the hard part. The professional must decide which keywords to utilize in the campaign and which keywords to delete. To delete a keyword, a professional needs to highlight the keyword and press the delete key.

All remaining keywords are assessed by the Google search engine, but not to the same extent. The professional can control which searches trigger an ad by specifying the match "type" for each keyword. There are three positive match types: broad match, phrase match, and exact match. Each is described below followed by a discussion of negative match types.

The Broad Match option may show an ad on searches that are related to the keyword, which can include searches that do not contain the keyword terms. This helps attract more visitors to the professional's website, spend less time building keyword lists, and focus your spending on keywords that work. Broad match is the default match type that all keywords are assigned as if the professional did not specify another match type (exact match, phrase match, or a negative match type). To help deliver relevant matches, this match type may also take into account the following:

- The user's recent search activities
- The content of the landing page
- Other keywords in an ad group to better understand keyword intent

The Phrase Match option may show an ad on searches that include the meaning of the keyword. The meaning of the keyword can be implied, and user searches can be a more specific form of the meaning. Phrase match is more targeted than the default broad match option, but is more flexible than exact match. With phrase match, you can reach more customers, while still showing your ads to customers who are most likely searching for your product or service. The syntax for phrase match is to put quotes around the keyword, such as "real estate lawyer."

Exact Match is the Google keyword match type that allows a professional to show an ad when a searcher types the exact word or phrase the professional has bid on. An Exact Match keyword in Google Ads will only enter an auction in which the search query perfectly matches or is a close variant of your keyword. The syntax for exact match is to put brackets around the keyword, [real estate lawyer in Chicago].

There is another type of keyword that has to be discussed – the negative keyword. Negative keywords let a professional exclude search terms from a campaign and help the professional focus on only the keywords that matter to real estate prospects.

Negative match types must me contrasted with the positive match types discussed above. One key to a highly targeted campaign is choosing what not to target. When selecting negative keywords for search campaigns, look for search terms that are similar to a professional's keywords, but might cater to users searching for a different product.

For search campaigns, a professional can use broad match, phrase match, or exact match negative keywords. However, these negative match types work differently than their positive counterparts. The main difference is that the professional will need to add synonyms, singular or plural versions, misspellings, and other close variations if you want to exclude them.

Negative broad match is the default for negative keywords. For negative broad match keywords, a professional's ad would not show if the search included *all* the negative keyword terms, even if the terms are in a different order. The ad may still show if the search contains only *some* of the keyword terms.

For example, negative broad match keyword: running shoes

Search	Could an ad show?
blue tennis shoes	✓
running shoe	✓
blue running shoes	✗
shoes running	✗
running shoes	✗

For negative phrase match keywords, a professional's ad would not show if the search included the exact keyword terms in the same order. The search may include additional words, but the ad would not show as long as all the keyword terms are included in the search in the same order. The search may also include additional characters to a word and the ad will show even when the rest of the keyword terms are included in the search in the same order.

For example, negative phrase match keyword: "running shoes"

Search	Could an ad show?
blue tennis shoes	✓

running shoe ✓

blue running shoes ✗

shoes running ✓

running shoes ✗

For negative exact match keywords, a professional's ad would not show if the search included the exact keyword terms, in the same order, without extra words. Your ad may still show if the search contains the keyword terms with additional words.

For example, negative exact match keyword: [running shoes]

Search	Could an ad show?
blue tennis shoes	✓
running shoe	✓
blue running shoes	✓
shoes running	✓
running shoes	✗

Symbols can be important in negative keyword strategy. A professional can use three symbols, ampersands (&), accent marks (á), and asterisks (*) in negative keywords. Negative keywords with accent marks are considered two different negative keywords, like sidewalk cafe and sidewalk café. Similarly, "socks & shoes" is different than "socks and shoes".

Here are some of the symbols that Google does NOT recognize:

Ignored symbols: A professional can add periods (.) to the list of negative keywords, but these will be ignored. That means the keywords Fifth Ave. and Fifth Ave, for example, are considered identical negative keywords. If a professional adds pluses (+) to the negative keywords they will usually be ignored (for example blue+car), however in some cases if a + is at the end of a word (for example C++) it will not be ignored.

Invalid symbols: A professional should see an error message if he/she adds negative keywords that contain certain symbols. Some of the symbols that cannot be used as negative keywords are: , ! @ % ^ () = {} ; ~ ` <> ? \ |.

Site and search operators: The "site:" operator will be removed from the negative keywords. That means if a professional adds the negative keyword [site:www.example.com dark chocolate], it will be considered the same as [dark chocolate]. Search operators will also be ignored. For example, if a professional adds the search operator "OR" to the negative keyword dark chocolate, like "OR dark chocolate," the "OR" command will be ignored, and the negative keyword will be just dark chocolate.

Other search operators: Adding a minus (-) operator to the front of a keyword will cause this keyword to be ignored for negative keyword matching. For example, if you have a negative keyword "dark -chocolate", it'll be considered the same as just "dark".

Negative keywords can be tricky to implement. Choose negative keywords carefully. If a professional uses too many negative keywords, ads might reach fewer customers. Negative keywords do not match to close variants so ads might still show on searches or pages that contain close variations of negative keyword terms. Also remember that there is no negative broad match modifier match type. Finally, a professional's ad might still show when someone searches for a phrase that is longer than 16 words, and the negative keyword follows that 16th word.

The selection of the keywords and the match types completes the ad group set up page. The professional should click the blue "Save and Continue" button on the bottom of the page to continue creating the campaign.

c. Ad Creation

Ad creation is the most visually appealing step in creating a campaign because of the Google Ads interface, which superimposes a professional's ad text over both a simulated cell phone and a simulated desktop monitor. The phone and desktop monitor dynamically adjust as the professional changes headlines and descriptions. Google Ads also shows a circular "Ad strength" meter to help a professional gage the effectiveness of proposed text. The Google ad tool suggests various headlines and descriptions that can be change as needed by the professional. Click the blue "Save and Continue" button at the bottom of the page after the professional is satisfied with the created ad.

d. Billing

A professional has to create a billing account if one has not already been created. If created, Google will automatically display the type of credit card (Visa/Mastercard/etc.) and the last four digits of the credit card number. To complete the campaign set up, the professional clicks the blue "Submit" button. Note that Google will charge the professional every 30 days or when the professional reaches the monthly billing threshold established by the professional while creating the campaign, whichever comes first.

The professional has the option to cancel or delete the campaign prior to submitting it. To do so, the professional clicks on the professional's picture in the upper, right-hand corner of the screen to reveal the Google Ads account number and status. To the right of the status is a recycle icon that removes the Google Ads account.

Google Ad Auction

Google search results appear in a nanosecond after a Google query is entered, but what is behind the scenes that determines the ad results and the ranking of those ad results? Every time an ad appears, it goes through what Google calls the ad auction, a process that decides which ads will appear and in which order (or whether any ads will meet the minimum required Ad Rank necessary to show at all). It is not like an art auction where the highest bidder always wins; instead, Google Ads goes through the four steps discussed below.

First, Google accepts the query entered into the Google search engine, like "Denver tax lawyer." Second, Google narrows the possible results. The Google Ads system finds all ads whose keywords match the search phrase "Denver tax lawyer" closely enough. From that set of matching ads, the system ignores any that are not eligible, like ads that target a different country or are disapproved.

Third, Google narrows the subset of possible ads by removing certain ads from consideration. The system then determines which ads have a sufficiently high Ad Rank to show (for example, do the ads have a sufficiently high expected click-through rate, and will the ads and landing pages provide a good user experience). Ads that do not exceed the minimum quality standards necessary to show are also removed.

Fourth, the remaining ads are shown, ordered on the page based on Ad Rank, a combination of bid amount, the quality of your ads and landing page, the Ad Rank thresholds, the context of the person's search, and the expected impact of extensions and other ad formats.

The most important thing to remember is that the auction process uses the professional's ad's Ad Rank to determine its position. So even if the competition bids higher than the professional, the professional can still win a higher position -- at a lower price -- with high-quality ads and landing pages.

Also remember that the auction process repeats for every search on Google, each time with potentially different results depending on the competition at that moment and which ad the professional uses. So do not worry if the professional's position on the page fluctuates – it is normal for it to vary each time.

Keyword Bidding Strategies

Optimizing keyword bidding should be the goal of all professionals. The effectiveness of running a Google Ads Search campaign depends to a large degree on the success of keyword bidding. A professional does not want to bid to little money on a keyword that the professional's ads no not appear on a Google search. However, the professional does not want to over-bid in an effort to get his/her ads to appear on a Google search. The sweet spot is a bid just high enough so that the ad appears but no more than that. Unfortunately, it is not an exact science and requires expertise or lots of trial and error.

A professional's bid strategy is to optimize bids to meet advertising goals. Manual bidding requires a professional to set a maximum cost-per-click bid for ad groups or keywords. Automated bid strategies set bids based on the professional's goals. A professional has six automated bid strategies to choose from and each is described below: Target CPA, Target ROAS, Maximize Clicks, Maximize Conversions, Maximize Conversion Value, and Target Impression Share.

Target CPA is a Google Ads Smart Bidding strategy that sets bids to help get as many conversions as possible at or below the target cost-per-action (CPA) set by a professional. It uses advanced machine learning to automatically optimize bids and offers auction-time bidding capabilities that tailor bids for each and every auction.

Target ROAS lets a professional bid based on a target return on ad spend ("ROAS"). This strategy helps a professional get more conversion value or revenue at the target return on the set ad spend. A professional's bids are automatically optimized at auction-time, allowing the professional to tailor bids for each auction. Target ROAS is available as either a standard strategy for a single campaign or a portfolio strategy across multiple campaigns.

Maximize Clicks is an automated bid strategy that sets a professional's bids to help get as many clicks as possible within the professional's budget. A professional can use Maximize Clicks for a single campaign or set it up as a portfolio bid strategy. Portfolio strategies group together multiple campaigns into a single strategy. The professional can set a cap on bids when using a Maximize Clicks bid strategy. It lets the professional control the maximum amount he/she is willing to pay for each click. If the professional does not enter a maximum CPC bid limit, Google Ads adjusts the bids to try to get the professional as many clicks as possible while spending the budget.

Maximize Conversions automatically sets bids to help get the most conversions for a professional's campaign while spending the budget. It uses advanced machine learning to automatically optimize bids and offers auction-time bidding capabilities that tailor bids for each and every auction. Bid adjustments allow a professional to show ads more or less frequently based on where, when, and how people search. Because Maximize Conversions helps optimize bids based on real-time data, a professional's existing bid adjustments are not used. There is one exception: a professional can still set mobile bid adjustments to -100%. Using historical information about the campaign and evaluating the contextual signals present at auction-time, Maximize Conversions bidding automatically finds an optimal bid for the professional's ad each time it is eligible to appear. It uses advanced machine learning to automatically optimize bids and offers auction-time bidding capabilities that tailor bids for each and every auction to help get the cheapest conversions available for your budget.

Maximize the total conversion value of a professional's campaign within the specified budget with the Maximize Conversion Value bidding strategy. This bidding strategy uses advanced machine learning to automatically optimize and set bids. It also offers auction-time bidding capabilities that tailor bids for each auction. The professional defines the value that the professional wants to maximize, such as sales revenue or profit margins, when setting up conversion tracking for the account. Bid adjustments allow the professional to show ads more or less frequently based on where, when, and how people search. Because Maximize Conversion Value helps optimize bids based on real-time data, the professional's existing bid adjustments are not used. There is one exception: a professional can still set mobile bid adjustments of -100%.

Target Impression Share is a Smart Bidding strategy that automatically sets bids with the goal of showing the ad on the absolute top of the page, on the top of the page, or anywhere on the page of Google search results. Target Impression Share is available either as a standard strategy in a single campaign or as a portfolio strategy across multiple campaigns. Target Impression Share bidding automatically sets bids to help achieve a professional's impression share goal across all campaigns using this strategy.

Keyword Ad Integration

The best search ads contain the very keywords the user imputed into the Google search engine. The user is subliminally influenced by the keywords appearing in the ad – which makes the ad appear more relevant that an ad not containing the keywords.

A professional should strive to cause the keywords to appear in several places, including:

- Ad headline
- Display URL
- Ad extensions

SECRET 17: FACEBOOK MARKETING

Facebook is the largest social media platform with a reported 2.7 billion monthly active users. Used by just about everyone in the world, Facebook recently hit the monumental milestone of recording one billion individual users in a single day. That means that one in every seven people logged into their Facebook profile in a single 24-hour period. That means that Facebook touched and connected in some way with every seventh person on Earth in a single day.

Facebook is an infinitely powerful tool. Given the sheer breadth and expanse of its user base, Facebook has for the first time in the history of civilization, given people and now businesses the opportunity to connect with virtually every adult person in America. From a business perspective, it is easy to fantasize about leveraging the powers and capabilities of Facebook to grow the firm. It is almost sinfully pleasurable to imagine that if only a professional could harness the powers of Facebook, every single person in a professional's target audience could theoretically be using the professional's services.

FREE MARKETING: FACEBOOK ACCOUNT

This writing assumes a professional knows how to create a Facebook account. It is also assumed a professional has created a Facebook post and shared a Facebook post.

Best practices suggest not using a professional's personal Facebook account for overt marketing purposes. A reminder to friends that the professional practices law is helpful when subtle and infrequent. Instead, a professional should create a separate Facebook Page to market his/her practice and add a post from the personal account that contains a link to the professional's Facebook Page.

FREE MARKETING: FACEBOOK PAGE AND POSTS

The first part of this Facebook discussion focuses on a professional's creation of a Facebook Page and posting best practices. This is free marketing and must be contrasted with paid advertising that will be discussed elsewhere.

Creating a Facebook Page

Facebook makes adding a Facebook Page easy and intuitive. A professional opens the personal Facebook account and navigates to the main menu and locates the "+" sign inside a grey circle immediately to the right of the user's picture and name. Click the "+" sign to reveal a submenu labeled "Create." One of the options is creating a "Page" by clicking on the word "Page" or the icon next to it.

The professional is linked to a "Create a Page" form where the professional is required to insert the Page name, Page category, and Page description. The Page name should be the name of the professional's firm. The Page category must be one of the pre-selected categories offered by Facebook. The professional cannot create his/her own category. Next, the professional must enter the description of the page in 255 characters of less. The professional should write about what the professional does, the services provided, or the purpose of the Facebook Page.

Facebook provides both a desktop preview and mobile preview image of what the Page will look like once the Page is created. The professional creates the Page by clicking the blue "Create Page" button at the bottom of the screen.

The created Page allows the professional to add an optional profile image. Best practices suggest adding the professional's photo. The photo should be taken by a professional photographer and be limited to a headshot. The professional is also given the option of adding a "cover photo" that represents what the Page is about.

The professional can add information about the professional practice, including the professional's phone number, email address, location, and business hours. A website address can be displayed and an "action" button can be used to link to the professional's website home page or a special landing page for Facebook visitors.

Posting Best Practices

Posting on the firm Page is a great way to let clients and prospects know what the professional is up to. First, the professional should share meaningful updates. Whether it is content related to law or updates on what the professional is doing, stay in touch with the target audience with Facebook posts. Use short, fun-to-read copy and eye-catching images to get attention. Second, the professional can get more attention for a special post by pinning it to the Page or embedding it in the professional's website. When the professional pins a post, it will remain at the top of the professional's Page so it is the first thing people will see. Third, the professional can promote news, special discounts, videos, or up-coming special events.

Follow the following checklist to create an effective Facebook post:

✓ Keep the focus on the value proposition – how are the professional's services going to help the prospective client?

✓ Create engaging and easy to understand content to post on Facebook that promotes a professional's service.

✓ Use both direct and indirect lead generation content to create posts.

✓ Set goals for each post – What are the professional's goals? What is the professional trying to accomplish? Is it more "likes," shares, comments, awareness, etc.?

✓ Use some sort of metric system to track clicks and leads generated.

✓ Include a decisive call to action in every single post – do not leave the user guessing what to do next.

✓ Use stimulating visuals – it will attract more users and increase engagement, clicks, and conversion rates.

✓ Make the landing pages perfect. These pages should be appealing, easy to understand, and instruct the user what to do next.

✓ Keep the text in the Facebook posts to fewer than 90 characters – otherwise it risks becoming truncated.

Likes

Before discussing how a professional can attract more clients using a Facebook Page, let us start out with the WHY. Why does a professional want to attract more "likes" on Facebook (hereinafter, "Likes")? Why is it that Facebook Likes attract more clients? There are three primary reasons, and each of them is equally critical to a professional's business and revenue.

The first reason that Facebook is critical to a professional's revenue is that quality Likes equal real relationships. There is a difference between having a lot of Facebook Page Likes and having a lot of quality Facebook

Page Likes. The latter is much superior. It is easier than a professional might think to simply get Facebook Page Likes. All it requires is a few dollars and some knowhow. These days, a professional can get thousands of Likes simply by buying them. Buying Likes is a façade. It simply gives the appearance that a Facebook Page is important or well followed when in fact it is not.

The effect will be that a professional's purchased fans will never Like or share any of a professional's posts. When this happens the engagement score will drop, and the damage is nearly irreversible. This defeats the purpose of getting Likes. However, a professional should seek to combine a large, quality fan base buttressed with corresponding Likes with strategies to engage in important discourse that fans care about. Professionals should position themselves as the fans go-to-source in the niche for a lot of people. Engaging in meaningful conversation will create trust and loyalty, and when the time is right, the Facebook fans will want to do business with the professional. It is simpler to convert Facebook Likes into leads when leads truly like and trust the professional.

The second reason that Facebook is critical to a professional's revenue is because quality fans equal lucrative leads. An often-overlooked benefit to building a robust and quality fan following is that a professional can more easily build an email list with quality subscribers who are eager to hear from the professional on a regular and ongoing basis. Using Facebook to build an email list of subscribers who actually want to hear from the professional is a great way to turn those Likes into tangible lucrative leads.

The third reason that Facebook is critical to a professional's revenue is that quality fans equal money saving marketing strategies. Facebook allows its users to run what is called a "fan-only" campaign. A fan-only marketing campaign allows the creator to create Facebook ads that will only be seen by a professional's existing fan base. The benefit is that it costs significantly less per click than ads that are directed to Facebook's general public. So, the benefit to the professional is that targeting the soon to be robust and meaningful fan base with directed advertisements will save the professional marketing dollars that can be earmarked for later campaigns or reassigned to other advertising initiatives.

How to Utilize Facebook

A professional needs direction and a clear and well thought out strategy to turn the professional's newly realized desire to attract quality Facebook Likes and fans into actual clients. The *how* is the hardest part. It requires critical reflection on identifying a professional's core business, the professional's audience, what type of content will drive lead generation, how to create and share that content on Facebook, and lastly, how to convert members of the virtual audience into tangible leads.

Prioritize Business Objectives

If a professional has created a Facebook Page, it is probably for the singular purpose of attracting more business. However, generating more business from Facebook will mean one thing for a firm for example, and something entirely different for a clothing store. Ultimately, this means that different businesses may have different objectives, such as: (1) driving in-office consultations; (2) increasing online traffic; (3) launching a new product or service; or (4) building brand awareness. Regardless of the business objective, if a professional wants to turn Facebook fans/Likes into paying clients, the professional first has to create an audience, direct incoming traffic to the website, convert each unique user into a tangible lead, and cultivate those online leads into actual customers.

Building a Facebook Audience

A professional will only be able to develop a loyal and engaged constituency of followers if the firm's Facebook Page is as discoverable on Facebook as it is off of Facebook. It is impossible for users to connect and Like a professional's business Page if they are unaware that the firm and its Facebook Page exists. Employ the following four tactics to make the firm's Facebook Page as discoverable and conspicuous as possible.

First, fill out all informational fields with searchable content. This means that once the Facebook Page has been created, make sure that the About section includes: (1) an overview of what the firm has to offer; (2) a link to the firm's website; and (3) other relevant information that will enable prospects to better understand how the firm can help them.

Second, invite existing contacts to Like the page. Simply ask existing clients, friends, and family to connect with the firm's Facebook Page by following and liking it. Also ask them to post positive reviews. Within the Page Manager section of the firm's Facebook profile, a professional can invite personal Facebook friends to Like the Page, share the Page with their Facebook friends through the newsfeed, or upload an existing list of email contacts to encourage them to connect as well. Use discretion and judgment when inviting contacts. Do not be "that guy" who invites all his contacts regardless of whether they may be interested in the Facebook Page. Remember, the quality of the contacts is more important that the quantity.

Third, make it known that the professional has a Facebook Page. Promote the professional's Facebook presence using all existing online and offline marketing channels that already exist. Make it easy for existing contacts and clients to Like the Page. Place stickers (i.e., the Facebook thumbs up "Like" sticker) in the firm's window promoting its Facebook Page and URL. Include the same social plugin on the website, blog, business card, direct mailings, and other marketing channels.

Fourth, build a Facebook audience by creating value for them. If a professional has a finger on the pulse of the common issues or questions shared by the professional's clients, then post content addressing or answering those issues or questions. A professional is creating value by providing answers while presenting oneself as the go-to authority on the subject.

Creating Content and Lead Generation Strategies

A professional's content and lead generation strategies should center around creating content that the audience will find useful and valuable. The goal is to provide content to the users through which the professional can create in them a sense of trust and loyalty. There are many mediums through which a professional can provide an audience with content. For example, a professional can create blog posts, webinars, podcasts, newsletters, eBooks, etc. By creating content accessible through various mediums, the professional can promote the firm in unique ways on Facebook.

For example, if a professional has written a blog article, take a passage from it that focuses on a specific point or issue that the professional anticipates will be of interest to the broader fan base. Use that passage to create a Facebook post that gives the audience an idea of what they will learn by reading the whole blog post. Make sure to paste the blog URL in the Facebook post. The objective is to get a professional's Facebook fans to follow the URL to the website.

An easy and effective way to conceptualize the purpose of Facebook posts is to think of them as digital breadcrumbs that draw the audience towards a more substantial piece of content. If the audience member wants to see the whole blog post, for example, then direct them to a landing page where after they input their contact information (e.g. email address) they will be directed to the blog post. This will deliver useful content to the reader and in return, the professional gets a solid and tangible lead.

Creating and Sharing Content on Facebook to Drive Lead Generation

The goal is to generate leads through content shared on Facebook. The most effective way to do this is by sharing diverse content that addresses goals other than generating leads or driving sales.

The cardinal rule of posting content to Facebook is that posts should not be sales driven. When a firm only posts sales driven content, it comes off as too forced and self-righteous. The better way is to generate leads both directly and indirectly by sharing a varied mix of content. Direct lead generation results from sharing content that directs the user to a landing page on the website where the user can only access the content after filling out a contact form. Examples of direct lead generation include an eBook, template, checklist, or blog post.

Indirect lead generation results from sharing freely accessible information that is immediately consumable and that will ultimately generate a lead. Examples of indirect lead generation include photos, third party content, and event invites.

Initially, it might seem like a waste of time and resources, aiming for more nebulous goals such as reach, awareness, and buzz, as well as increased fan engagement through comments, Likes, and shares. These fluffier goals are a direct link to customer engagement which will result in more clients. The most effective way to increase customer engagement is by posting a balanced but varied assortment of direct and indirect lead generation content. The goal is to capture the fan's attention. Only once a professional has captured their attention, can the professional get them to click links or Like posts, which will ultimately drive traffic, increase leads, and improve conversion rates.

Despite the fact that every brand on Facebook is there for the sole purpose of attracting more clients, each post should serve an important purpose and further an overarching goal. This is why indirect lead generation posts are equally as important as direct lead generation posts. The goal may be to encourage more comments on posts or expand the breadth of a professional's message by increasing how many users share the posts. The point is that the professional needs leads to get clients. Getting leads means making the brand more visible on Facebook which can only be done by focusing on those fluffier goals – comments, Likes, and shares. Increased visibility will drive more traffic to the website and generate more quality leads.

Converting Members of a Virtual Audience into Tangible Leads

It used to be that marketers could reach their target audience for free by posting an update and that update would appear in their intended user's timeline. This is no longer the case. As Facebook has grown, it has evolved from a free or low-cost platform to a paid marketing platform. As Facebook's user base has grown over the years, a brand's ability to reach their intended fan base/market has diminished. Now, there is more competition than ever among brands competing to appear in a user's confined News Feed.

During any single moment, there are thousands of stories and posts fighting to appear in a News Feed. Facebook's algorithm prioritizes them in such a way that only about 20% of them get published to the News Feed. This means that a professional has to be willing to pay handsomely when the professional wants to ensure that a post appears on a target audience's news feed. Marketers are no longer able to organically grow their business; you have to pay to play.

If a professional is going to pay handsomely to make sure that the posts reach the intended users, then the professional better make sure that what is being posted is effective and is going to capture the attention of the audience. Step one in deciding what to advertise is identifying the goal or objective of a particular post. If the goal is to drive traffic, leads, and customers, then the post must include a link back to the website. Facebook actually lets a professional test the effectiveness of the post prior to publishing it on the Facebook Page. A professional can create "dark posts" which appear in the News Feed but not on a Page. Since dark posts do not appear on a Page, a professional can create an infinite number of targeted advertisements and subsequently determine which advertisement is most effective prior to sharing it on the Page. Doing this allows a professional to test the efficacy of the post without disrupting the professional's entire fan base.

PAID ADVERTISING

Paid advertising should be a key component of a professional's Facebook marketing strategy. Paid advertising includes simple Facebook "boosted" posts, Facebook promotions, and complex Facebook ads.

Boosted Posts

A boosted post is a post to a professional's timeline that the professional can apply money to in order to boost it to an audience of the professional's choosing. When a professional boosts a post, it will show up in the professional's audience's Facebook News Feed as an ad.

Boosting a post is the simplest way to advertise on Facebook. Boosted posts differ from Facebook ads because they are not created in Ads Manager and do not have all of the same customization features. The "boosting" process empowers a professional to determine interests, age, and gender for ad targeting. This helps the professional reach people who most likely need professional services.

The professional can choose any post that is already present on the professional's Page timeline and boost it. When the professional boosts a post, three things must be identified. First, the professional must specify the target audience to be reached. Second, the professional must state a maximum budget to spend over the course of the entire campaign. Third, the professional must declare how long the ad should run. Once the ad is approved, Facebook users in the professional's target audience will see the boosted post in their News Feeds for the duration of the campaign.

How to Boost a Post

Post boosting is easy. A blue "Boost Post" button appears at the bottom of a Facebook Page post. Clicking the button links the professional to an ad interface page that allows the professional to select a targeted audience, identify the duration of the boosted post, and set a total budget for the boost post. Facebook offers an ad preview that shows what the ad will look like. Facebook also estimates the daily results of people reached and post engagement. The post is ready to be boosted once the professional inserts all the information into the ad interface. All the professional has to do then is click the blue "Boost Post Now" button at the bottom of the interface.

Facebook Promotions

Facebook promotions are a subset of Facebook Ads and are created directly from a professional's Facebook Page. Promotions are only available on Facebook Pages. That contrasts with Facebook ads that are created in Ads Manager.

Facebook promotions are one of the fastest ways to create an ad on Facebook since in most cases, Facebook will automatically suggest text and images for the ad from information entered by the professional in the Facebook Page. These images, videos, and text can be changed by the professional.

To begin, click the blue "Promote" button on the bottom of the Facebook Page to be linked to the "Choose a Goal" page. There, the professional must choose the promotion objective from seven choices: Get Started with Automated Ads; Build Your Business, Get More Website Visitors, Get More Leads, Boost a Post, Get More Messages, and Promote Your Page.

A professional should consider selecting the "Get More Website Visitors" option which links the professional to the

"Promote Your Website" page. There, the professional sees an ad preview suggested by Facebook with an image and text pulled from the professional's Page. The professional has the option of accepting or replacing the ad text. An "automatic enhancement" toggle button allows Facebook to automatically adjust the ad for each person viewing the ad. This may include adjusting image brightness and contrast, showing the original aspect ratio if Facebook thinks it is likely to perform better.

Next, the professional can create the media image for the ad by accepting the image Facebook pulled from the Page or uploading an image. Multiple images can be downloaded to create a carousel. Videos can be downloaded for extra impact.

Facebook allows the professional the ability to create the ad headline, with the default being a truncated version of the professional's Facebook Page name. The promotion section offers a button linking the ad to the professional's website home page. The linked website address is taken by default from the professional's Page but can be changed to a special landing page for Facebook users. The button label can be changed to any one of 11 choices – the default is "Apply Now." Best practices suggest changing the button to "Learn More" or "Contact Us."

Choosing the audience for the ad is a vital step for cost effective advertising. Facebook allows a professional to choose a target audience based on location, age, gender, and interest of people. Facebook provides an estimated number of people reached by the ad based on the target audience parameters set by the professional – plus a visual meter with an indicator moving between "Specific" and "Broad."

The Facebook interface allows the professional to select the minimum and maximum age of the people who will find the ad relevant. In addition, the interface grants the professional the ability to pinpoint a location in which the ad may appear. For example, the professional can choose the whole United States, the State(s) in which the professional is licensed, a particular county or city in which the professional practices, or even the street on which the professional's office is located. The location interface also allows for targeting beyond the specified location anywhere from one to 50 miles.

More detailed targeting features are available providing the professional with flexibility to reach people based on demographics, interests, and behaviors. Best practices suggest that market research should be done before the professional spends his/her limited marketing budget. Demographic categories and subcategories include the following:

- Education
  - School
  - Field of study
- Financial
  - income
- life events
  - anniversary
    - anniversary within 30 days
    - anniversary within 31-60 days
  - away from family
  - away from hometown
  - birthday
    - birthday month
    - upcoming birthday
  - friends of
    - men with a birthday in 0-7 days
    - men with a birthday in 7-30 days
    - recently moved
    - women with a birthday in 0-7 days

- women with a birthday in 7-30 days
- newly engaged people
- newlyweds
- people with birthdays in a month
- people with birthdays in a week
  - long-distance relationship
  - new job
  - new relationship
  - newly engaged (1 year)
  - newly engaged (3 months)
  - newly engaged (6 months)
  - newlywed (1 year)
  - newlywed (3 months)
  - newlywed (6 months)
  - recently moved
- parents
  - new parents (0-12 months)
  - all parents
  - with adult children (18-26 years)
  - with early school-age children (6-8 years)
  - with preschoolers (3-5 years)
  - with preteens (9-12 years)
  - with teenagers (13-17 years)
  - with toddlers (1-2 years)
- relationship
  - civil union
  - complicated
  - divorced
  - domestic partnership
  - engaged
  - in a relationship
  - married
  - open relationship

- o separated
- o single
- o unspecified
- o widowed
- work
  - o industries
    - administrative services
    - architecture and engineering
    - arts, entertainment, sports, and media
    - business and finance
    - cleaning and maintenance services
    - community and social services
    - computation and mathematics
    - construction and extraction
    - education and libraries
    - farming, fishing, and forestry
    - food and restaurants
    - governmental employees (Global)
    - healthcare and medical services
    - IT and technical services
    - installation and repair services
    - legal services
    - life, physical and social sciences
    - management
    - military (Global)
    - production
    - protective services
    - sales
    - transportation and moving
    - veterans
  - o employers
  - o job Titles

The professional must identify the ad duration. Facebook's default is a continuous ad that never ends (or at least until the professional runs out of money). Best practices suggest clicking the radio button titled "Choose when this ad will end" and selecting a limited number of days. This practice is especially practical while the professional is testing ad effectiveness with A/B testing.

The Final step is to indicate the daily budget and click the blue "Promote Now" button to activate the campaign.

Facebook Ads

Facebook ads are created through Ads Manager and offer more advanced customization solutions. Ads Manager helps create, manage, and analyze a professional's Facebook ads in a single location.

There are many advertising objectives to help a professional reach specific business goals and the audiences the professional cares about most. Facebook ads can be optimized for website conversions, video views, shop orders and more, while a boosted post may initially be optimized for Page Likes, comments, and shares or overall brand awareness. Plus, Facebook ads provide a professional with the flexibility to choose ad placement in Facebook News Feed side ads, Messenger ads, Instagram stories, instant articles, and Audience Network.

A professional can maintain creative control over the ad creation process by utilizing Ads Manager. The professional can design an ad that fits the professional's goals, including creating a carousel ad, adding specific descriptions, and adding a call-to-action button to drive the audience to take action. These are only a few of the creative and formatting options available in Ads Manager that are not available when boosting a post from the professional's Facebook Page.

Ads Manager allows a professional to use advance targeting capabilities not available with boosted posts. Boosting posts let the professional decide on interests, age, and gender for your ad targeting. This helps reach people who most likely care about professional services. With Facebook ads, the professional can use more advanced tools to create overlapping audience types, lookalike audiences and more.

Ads Manager

A professional's Ads Manager account can be accessed one of two ways. Once logged into Facebook, a professional can open a new browser window and type https://www.facebook.com/ads/ manager into the search bar. Alternatively, the professional can reach Ads Manager from the professional's Facebook Page by clicking the left sidebar menu item labeled "All Ads" to be linked to the "View Results" page. There, the professional can link to the Ads Manager page by clicking on the phrase "Show more details in Ads Manager" appearing at the bottom of the page. The link takes the professional to the Facebook Account page that sorts the professional's ads by campaign, ad set, and ad.

Click the green "+ Create" button on the top menu to create a new ad. Alternatively, click the grey "Create Ad" button at the bottom of the page to create a new ad. Once clicked, the professional is linked to a "Choose a Campaign Objective" dialogue box that presents the professional with three alternative campaign objectives:

- Awareness
  - o Brand awareness
  - o Reach

- Consideration
  - Traffic
  - Engagement
  - App installs
  - Video views
  - Lead generation
  - Messages
- Conversion
  - Conversions
  - Catalog sales
  - Store traffic

Best practices suggest that a professional would select the Consideration/Traffic radio button when the objective is to send prospects to the professional's website homepage or landing page. Next, the professional should name the campaign, name the ad set, and name the first ad.

A campaign budget can be set by clicking the "Show More Options" dropdown menu arrow and the box next titled "Add Campaign Spending Limit." A new field is revealed in which the professional can set a dollar limit.

Clicking the blue "Next" box at the page bottom links the professional to the "Ad Set" interface screen.

Facebook "Ad Set"

The Ad Set interface screen gives the professional the option of creating his/her own ad or getting Facebook's assistance in creating ads from Facebook's "Dynamic Creative" tool – by clicking the toggle bar to the "on" position. The Dynamic Creative tool provides creative elements, such as images and headlines, and automatically generates combinations optimized for the professional's audience. Variations may include different formats or templates based on one or more elements.

The same interface allows the professional to create a special offer to drive more conversions, AKA Offer Advertising. The professional must select the Facebook account associated with the offer, and click the grey "Create Offer" button to reveal a "Create Offer" dialogue box. There, the professional enters the offer title and offer details along with the end date and time. Offer redemption comes next. The professional enters the online offer URL, promo code, total offers available, and any terms and conditions. Clicking the blue "Create" button at the bottom creates the offer ad.

Continuing down the Ad Set interface, the professional completes the "Budget & Schedule" section. The daily budget is identified as well as the scheduled start date and optional end date.

Next, the interface allows the professional to define the target audience. The first parameter is location. The interface allows the professional to select the United States, the State(s) in which the professional is licensed, a county, a city, or town. The interface also allows a professional to exclude portions of the location selected. For example, the professional could select DuPage County, IL but exclude that portion of Westmont, IL that is within DuPage County, IL.

The next audience parameter is age. The professional can pick a minimum and maximum age demographic. The gender parameter allows the professional to choose among three categories: men only, women only, or all genders.

The final parameter is "Detailed Targeting" of the professional's audience, which includes or excludes people from an audience based on criteria such as demographics, interests, and/or behaviors. These detailed targeting options may be based on many factors, including: ads users click; Pages with which users engage; activities users engage in on Facebook related to things like the users' device usage or travel preferences; demographics like age, gender and location; and the mobile device users use and the speed of their network connection.

The professional starts detailing the audience by adding demographics, interests, or behaviors. Facebook provides a field to insert the professional's suggestion and a "Browse" feature that, when clicked, reveals a dropdown menu of demographics, interests, and behaviors – each with an accordion arrow for further subcategories. Adding more targeting details here will expand the professional's audience to include more people. The details a professional selects are not mutually inclusive. This means that if the professional adds three interests (for example, movies, books and TV), Facebook will look for people who match the location, age, gender and language the professional selected, who also match with either "movies," or "books" or "TV."

The Facebook defined categories are as follows:

- Demographics
  - Education
    - Education level
      - Further subgroups available
    - Fields of study
    - Schools
    - Undergrad Years
  - Financial
    - Income
      - Household income: top 5% of ZIP codes

- Household income: top 10% of ZIP codes
- Household income: top 10% - 25% of ZIP codes
- Household income: top 25% - 50% of ZIP codes

o Life Events
  - Anniversary
    - Within 30 days
    - Within 31-60 days
  - Away from family
  - Away from hometown
  - Birthday
    - Further subgroups available
  - Friends of …
    - men with a birthday in 0-7 days
    - men with a birthday in 7-30 days
    - recently moved
    - women with a birthday in 0-7 days
    - women with a birthday in 7-30 days
    - newly engaged people
    - newlyweds
    - people with birthdays in a month
    - people with birthdays in a week
  - Long-distance relationship
  - New job
  - New relationship

- Newly engaged (1 year)
- Newly engaged (3 months)
- Newly engaged (6 months)
- Newlywed (1 year)
- Newlywed (3 months)
- Newlywed (6 months)
- Recently moved

o Parents
- All parents
  - new parents (0-12 months)
  - all parents
  - with adult children (18-26 years)
  - with early school-age children (6-8 years)
  - with preschoolers (3-5 years)
  - with preteens (9-12 years)
  - with teenagers (13-17 years)
  - with toddlers (1-2 years)

o Relationship
- Relationship Status
  - civil union
  - complicated
  - divorced
  - domestic partnership
  - engaged
  - in a relationship
  - married
  - open relationship
  - separated

- single
- unspecified
- widowed

o Work
  - Employers
  - Job Titles
  - Industries
    - administrative services
    - architecture and engineering
    - arts, entertainment, sports, and media
    - business and finance
    - cleaning and maintenance services
    - community and social services
    - computation and mathematics
    - construction and extraction
    - education and libraries
    - farming, fishing, and forestry
    - food and restaurants
    - governmental employees (Global)
    - healthcare and medical services
    - IT and technical services
    - installation and repair services
    - legal services

- life, physical and social sciences
- management
- military (Global)
- production
- protective services
- sales
- transportation and moving
- veterans

Some of these categories are broad and embrace a large audience. A professional may want to narrow the audience to be more targeted in his/her marketing approach. Thankfully, Facebook has considered that and added a grey "Narrow Audience" button immediately below the chosen demographic. But note that the button does not appear until the professional chooses a demographic. Narrowing the audience helps Facebook focus the audience makeup on people who must match at least one of the professional's previously identified qualities and the additional details you add. For example, if the professional originally choses to include people who match with "movies," or "books" or "TV," and then narrows the search by adding "yoga," Facebook would then search for people who must match "yoga" and either "movies," "books" or "TV."

The professional can further refine the target audience by utilizing Facebook's "Exclude people who match" feature. New details can be chosen to exclude people from the audience previously selected. Each new option entered into the "exclude" field will decrease the size of the professional's audience.

The "Audience" section of the interface concludes with a grey "Save This Audience" button, which saves all of the audience parameters entered by the professional. By saving the audience, the professional can use the same demographics in future campaigns without having to reinvent the wheel.

The next section of the Ad Set interface is titled "Optimization & Delivery" and appears directly below the "Audience" section of the interface. The professional is given several options to optimize the ad delivery. A grey pulldown menu gives the professional four choices to optimize: Landing Page Views, Link Clicks, Daily Unique Reach, and Impressions. Landing Page Views delivers the professional's ads to people who are more likely to click on the ad's link and load the website. Link Clicks delivers the professional's ads to the people most likely to click on the link. Daily Unique Reach delivers the professional's ads to people up to once per day. Impressions delivers a professional's ads to people as many times as possible.

When the professional selects the Optimization for Ad Delivery option for an ad set, the professional is telling Facebook to get the intended result as efficiently as possible. In other words, the optimization choice is the desired outcome that Facebook's system bids on in the ad auction. For example, if the professional optimizes an ad set for link clicks, the ad set is targeted to people in the professional's audience who are most likely to click the ads' links.

Based on the optimization the professional chooses, the delivery system uses machine learning to improve each ad's performance and minimize the cost per optimization event. The optimization of the ad set can be different from the campaign objective. For example, the professional can choose conversions as the campaign objective, but optimize for link clicks within an ad set.

Keep in mind that some optimization events may require more budget than others (for example, a conversion may cost more than a landing page view). Therefore, it is important to consider the optimization choice when selecting the budget and bid strategy. Make sure the budget is large enough to accommodate the cost of the chosen optimization event. A good general rule is that the daily budget should be at least 10 times the average cost of the optimization event. For example, if the professional is optimizing for link clicks and the average cost per link click is $5, the daily budget should be at least $50. If the professional does not want to increase the budget, then he/she can try optimizing for an event that is higher up in the marketing funnel (for example, landing page views instead of conversions). Also, make sure the professional has set the bid cap or cost cap high enough to achieve the chosen optimization event. The bid cap is the maximum amount the professional is willing to bid to win in auctions and get the result for which the professional is optimizing. The cost cap is the average amount the professional wants to pay for the optimization event.

Facebook offers the professional an optional "Cost Control" feature. Set a cost control if the professional has a specific cost goal. When the field is left blank, Facebook's ad system will focus on spending the entire budget and getting the most results. By setting a cost control, the professional is telling Facebook which results to spend budget on. The Cost Control feature provides a field in which a dollar amount can be specified. If an amount is specified, then Facebook will aim to get the most optimized events (Landing Page Views, Link Clicks, Daily Unique Reach, or Impressions) and try to keep the average cost below the cost control amount specified by the professional using the cost cap bid strategy. Some results may cost more, and some may cost less. For example, assume the professional selects Landing Page Views as the optimized event and inserts $10 into the Cost Control field. In that case, Facebook will aim to get the most landing page views and try to keep the average cost below $10.00 using the cost cap bid strategy.

Facebook "Ad" Creation

The "Ad" interface requires multiple inputs. The professional must insert a unique name in the "Ad Name" field. Also, the professional must identify the Facebook Page associated with the ad by clicking on the pulldown menu arrow contained in the "Identity" section of the interface. Facebook provides a prepopulated set of the professional's Page(s).

The next section of the interface is the "Ad Setup" section. There, the professional can choose a format to structure the ad. Three radio button options are presented: single image or video; carousel; and collection. The single image or video radio button is the default.

The "Ad Creative" section is the next section of the interface. The professional uploads a media selection by clicking the grey "Add Media" button. The media can be picture(s) or video(s). Next, the professional tells people what the ad is about by including text in the "Primary Text" field. The primary text appears above the picture. Note that the primary text will be truncated by Facebook if too long. Facebook truncates the text and automatically adds a link at the end of the truncated text labeled "…See More." Best practices suggest maximizing the impact of the displayed text to entice the user to click on the ad, and not expect the user to be interested enough to click for more information. Facebook users do not search for ad information so make it easy on the user and give it to them in one shot. The professional can enter up to five different versions of the primary text – each to be used by Facebook on a random basis for optimization purposes.

Facebook allows the professional to add a short "Headline" for the ad. The headline appears below the picture. Note that the headline text will be truncated by Facebook if too long. Facebook truncates the text and adds an ellipsis ("...") at the end of the truncated text. Best practices suggest maximizing the impact of the displayed text to entice the user to click on the ad, and not expect the user to be interested enough to click for more information. The professional can enter up to five different versions of the headline – each to be used by Facebook on a random basis for optimization purposes.

Next, Facebook allows the professional to add a "Description" for the ad. The description appears below the headline. Note that the headline text will be truncated by Facebook if too long. Facebook truncates the text and adds an ellipsis ("...") at the end of the truncated text. Best practices suggest maximizing the impact of the displayed text to entice the user to click on the ad, and not expect the user to be interested enough to click for more information. Facebook users do not search for ad information so make it easy on the user and give it to them in one shot. The professional can enter up to five different versions of the description – each to be used by Facebook on a random basis for optimization purposes.

"Destination" is the next section of the "Ad Creative" interface. The destination determines what happens when the Facebook user clicks on the ad. The professional has three radio buttons from which to choose: Website, Facebook Event, Phone Call. A website URL must be inserted if the professional chooses the "website" radio button. A Facebook event URL must be entered if the professional chooses the

Facebook Event radio button. A phone number and country code must be entered if the professional chooses the Phone Call radio button. If the professional selects the Website radio button, then a "Call to Action" feature becomes available. The professional can select one of 19 call to action phrases to be inserted into a button appearing at the bottom of the ad. This call-to-action button links the Facebook user to the professional's website home page or landing page.

Facebook offers visual previews of multiple ad variations displaying the proposed ad in different formats. A professional can see how the ad would be displayed in a Facebook news feed, Groups feed, Facebook Marketplace, and more. Finally, the professional activates the finalized ad by clicking the green "Publish" button at the bottom of the Ad Creative interface.

Conclusion

In conclusion, Facebook is an extremely powerful marketing tool. With a Facebook Page and some thoughtful content, a professional has the power to target an infinitely large audience and actually convert them from digital leads into paying clients. Facebook's value is in its user base. Now more than ever, it is easier for professionals to cost effectively connect with other businesses and individuals. This means direct access to a growing audience.

PART 2: INDEX

Index

INDEX

Accountant..1, 67
accurate 101
Ad creation..224
Ad Creative..259, 260
ad groups 205, 217, 226
Ads Manager 242, 243, 247, 248
advertising10, 11, 15, 16, 17, 18, 19, 48, 99, 101, 102, 103,
    104, 105, 107, 109, 112, 133, 146, 147, 149, 166, 181, 182,
    183, 185, 186, 197, 200, 201, 203, 204, 209, 212, 226, 232,
    236, 241, 244, 248
Advertising10, 15, 99, 100, 102, 104, 105, 127, 129, 130, 132,
    134, 135, 138, 139, 180, 181, 250
advertising limitations 99, 105
aged 45-54 ....25, 26
alimony..8, 23, 29, 65
Animation 189, 195
Apprehension 36
attract more business 234, 236
average gross income 29
Bankruptcy Code10, 106, 107, 127, 129, 130, 132, 134, 135,
    138, 139, 155
BANKRUPTCY FILINGS BY STATE 39
Behavioral marketing...................................15, 20
billing..205, 209, 216, 224
boosted post 241, 242, 248
Boosting a post 242
brochure marketing 147, 148, 149, 153
Brochure marketing 9, 15, 147

272